The Shot and Beer Manager
Success Made Simple

Al Uhryniak

The Shot and Beer Manager
Success Made Simple
Copyright 2018
Al Uhryniak

All Rights Reserved
No portion of this publication may be reproduced, stored in any electronic system, or transmitted in any form or by any means, electronic, mechanical, photocopy, recording, or otherwise, without written permission from the author. Brief quotations may be used in literary reviews.

ISBN-13: 978-1720464297
ISBN-10: 1720464294

Dedicated to my dad and grandfather who had the shot and beer mentality of working hard for what you wanted, being direct, being kind but firm, taking responsibility for your own actions and always being decisive about doing what you believed was right.

And to my wife, who has been at my side guiding, encouraging and sharing our hopes and dreams our entire life together.

ACKNOWLEDGEMENTS

Special thanks to my family and our friend and neighbor Mary Ann Hume who all offered many suggestions to make this a better book. I only wish I would have incorporated all of their suggestions into the final version. Also, thanks to those good managers who throughout my working years were instrumental in teaching me how to be the best at whatever I was doing. And certainly, thanks to those many poor managers who I worked for and with over the years for demonstrating exactly what poor management was all about. All of you have contributed much to getting me to the place I'm in today.

Table of Contents

Preface   7
     Is There a Reason to Read This?
The Readers Frame of Mind   11
     How Does This Mindset Work?
First Things First – A Life Plan   15
     How and Why to Have a "Future" Roadmap
Setting the Stage   27
     How Do I Control My Path?
Your Frist Job   33
     Your Objective is More Than Money
The One Man Show   39
     But I Don't Want to Work for Someone Else
Your Management Responsibility   47
     Taking Care of Business
The Small Business Operation   59
     Is This Going to Work?
Managing Managers   69
     Being the Bad Guy
How to Approach Process Change   83
     Focus on The Necessity of Change?
Examples and Nuggets   97
     More Points to Remember
Time for a Shot and Beer?   109
     Wrap It

Preface

Every good book seems to have a Forward or Preface. It's intended to relate enough information so the casual browser can make an informed decision about the value of its content. So, in line with that I've written this preface. You're going to think this book isn't professional and written in a style like every business school book you've ever read. That's true. It's written in a down to earth style to cover common hurdles, be straight to the point and tell you what you need to know.

I called this "The Shot & Beer Manager" because in the world I grew up in it was an attitude: a straight forward way of looking at your life, work and people. It is a way of applying common sense, simple rules to what you do and how you act. You can go to business school or graduate from college and get your masters if you want to. Those are all good things. But, do they tell you how to actually conduct yourself and interact with all the people around you? Do they tell you how to take your knowledge and do what's necessary to make your life what you want it to be? Generally, the answer is "no". Many people graduate from schools every year and have the knowledge it takes to succeed, but they do not. They fall short when it comes to how to take that knowledge and take the steps to make decisions and take the actions necessary to make that knowledge work. It's not enough to know what to do. You have to know how to apply that knowledge and make your life and business come out the way you want. This book highlights ways to avoid the pitfalls most knowledgeable, smart people stumble over on their way to achieving far less than they could or should.

Now, this book is not intended for a "worker". If you're fine getting a job and working for some company your whole life then put this book down. This book is for someone who wants to run the show. Someone who wants to be at least a foreman, supervisor or small business owner. In many cases it positions you to start with that goal and exceed it to own or run a company or at least a department.

I've made an effort to skip any entry of a cliché or some psycho-babble statement meant only to make the author seem intelligent or "with-it". If that's the type of page filler you expect you will be disappointed. This book is intended to point out the steps to follow so you can take charge of your life and your job, assess situations, processes and make decisions that get things done. It's a roadmap for the do-er not the look-good, political, passive manager who only makes decisions once he knows which way the wind is blowing. If you want to be the passive manager find a book on kissing butt.

Many will find this book to be mean spirited. Many will say it's wrong to follow the points outlined here. They'll think it's a callous outlook. They'll say it's too hard, too complicated and comes across defining life in terms that don't take all the twists and turns into consideration. To that I say bullshit!

You're in charge of your life. If you want to reach the goal of the point on the horizon you've picked out for yourself it's hard work. What it takes to make it come out right is difficult, complicated and requires dedication to your goal. But, without a goal and the dedication to achieve it you are settling, settling for whatever "life" decides you can have. You have no goals, no objectives, no clear future for you or your family and no will to achieve your "point of the horizon".

If you don't want to be the person who settled for something less, adopt the shot and beer attitude and read the book.

This book assumes you are driving to your point on the horizon. The goal you have in mind is where you want to end up, what you want to have achieved in your personal and professional life. It's not written for the production line worker. It's not for the person who's point on the horizon is driven by being part of a workforce. No, this book is for the person who wants the house on the hill, the person who knows they'll do whatever it takes to get to the top. And the "top" is whatever goal they believe they will achieve no matter what it takes. So, by definition, it's not for everyone. No, this book is for the person who's committed to taking whatever action will be necessary to achieve their goals. The person who will not be satisfied unless they reach their version of their dream.

But please, don't confuse what I'm saying about doing whatever it takes to mean you can bend or break the rules. Absolutely not. It means you're willing to work long hours, even when you have other commitments, risk your money, make hard decisions, take chances and in short do whatever it takes to make things come out to match your plan. You are not being mean or heartless by taking this position and adopting the shot and beer attitude it will take. What you're doing is taking responsibility for not only driving to your goal but securing the future for everyone around you. As your personal life and work life are run to achieve your goals, you position the people around you to also achieve their goals. Never feel guilty about doing what's necessary to make your goal a reality.

    I've written this book from a guys' point of view because I'm a guy. It has no relationship to bias that pertains to gender, ethnic background or skin color. If you think those categories are somehow tied to how management people can succeed, put this book down. You obviously are not smart enough or open minded enough to understand the examples and nuggets found in this book.

The Readers Frame of Mind

First of all, if you're a person with letters after your name indicating you chose more than four extra years of schooling after high school....put this book down. I say that because many of you, but not all of you, do not have an inclination to decide what your point on the horizon is going to be. You will usually be found up front in the line to take credit when something has gone well. But you never want to be considered a "risk taker". You are not an innovator or a person who believes the risk of any well thought out plan outweighs the danger. And you never try anything unless you're sure it will work or reflect positively on you. You no doubt have a copy of your "diploma" hanging prominently on a wall at work and/or at home. You're most likely a person who finds more satisfaction in showing off qualification achievements than demonstrating actual accomplishments. You are a person so heavily influenced by people who claim to be smart (with no personal accomplishment proof) that no new information is going to make a difference in how you act. But I understand you might think it reflects well on you to have this book. So, if you feel obligated to show off a copy by placing it on your desk, a coffee table or in your bookcase I'm ok with that. But please don't quote from it as if you use its recommendations as tools in your life and management style.

    Next, if you felt the need to follow high school with an additional four years of schooling…..consider putting this book down. Clearly many of you can't think for yourself and made a decision to endure four extra years of what you never enjoyed or looked forward to when it was provided free of charge. For the most part you went for additional schooling because of the rumors of great parties and the fact that you wouldn't have to face reality for four more years. In addition, you somehow allowed yourself to believe that those extra four years would magically not only provide you better earning power but would justify a huge debt that would take you years to pay off. Now, I'm the first to acknowledge you probably relied heavily on parents and government grants to pay some or all of the bills. But this tricky little maneuver on your part doesn't mean you're smart, it just means you don't care who pays the price as long as you get what you want. Now, you have to assess for yourself if it really was the parties that attracted you to endure four years of college, or, was it the opportunity to meet a smart go getter who you might charm into being your spouse? Either of these categories have large ranks full of qualifying members. So, having said all that, if it applies to you, I'm forced to change my mind and say…..put the book down.

    Now we're left with those people who finished high school and were bold enough to just go face the world. It might be that you weren't bold but were just that blind to what the world had in store for you. You may have chosen a job, regardless of how menial, or you might have joined the armed forces (good for you). In either case you've seen a range of management styles and somewhere in that range is where you will personally find comfort.

You my friend are one of a rare breed who realized early, on purpose or by accident, that continuing on with schooling would only prove what you and everyone in your family already knew....you're not going to do well there. And, since there was no choice, you ventured into the mystical world of employment, offering no skills but a blank slate where any employer could create the employee of his/her choice. If you're in the position of looking at what is loosely considered "self-help" books, then you clearly are the person most likely to succeed. Nay, Nay, not most likely to succeed but certainly going to succeed because you've already realized the most important lesson of all...you and your life are what you choose to make it. You finally have at least the beginnings of a plan to get to a point on the horizon and intend to execute it. You my friend are going to read this book, find the nuggets most applicable to your situation and use them to move yourself into the position of your choice. That might be a position successfully working for someone else or hopefully to make a much better choice and create your own company. In either case, you will be one of the very rare people who can manage successfully, in any situation, and get things done. Many can manage but few, very few, can manage and actually get things done. Most passive managers today are satisfied taking credit for what the group would be able to do if no one provided any guidance or management function what-so-ever.

The world of business, just as life itself, is filled with people who don't know how to plan or make the decisions that get things done. Clearly, you've already realized your bosses could be doing so much better if they only handled situations differently. This book will give you the tools to evaluate life and work situations, processes and people. This will allow you to position those three pieces into a management style that gets things done. Your life and the entire business world should be driven by just one principle: do what it takes to achieve your goal effectively and efficiently with the highest quality. If you can do that your life will be what you hoped and planned; you'll make money and be successful at anything you do. You'll get to that point you picked out on your horizon.

First Things First....A Life Plan

Picking your point on the horizon doesn't just apply to work. You should be keenly aware of being in charge of your life. Not just while you're at work but all the time. It's a shot and beer style of managing that applies to everything you do. Because you have your objective you can focus on making things happen.....the objective is getting where you want to go. You're a person who can execute. It's not enough to make decisions, it's not enough to have a plan, it's not enough to look ahead and know where you want to be. Many more people can do that than can execute the plan. Having your end point can do that. And, executing a plan works best if you use the same approach in your personal life as you do for your work life.

Now before I go on let me just say while I talk about forming your life plan just as you leave high school or college, it can happen at any time. For a segment of the population that time comes years after high school or even college. I've known guys who drifted through college, got a job that seemed promising, and discovered some time later they were on a dead-end course. They had no chance of creating the type of life they imagined for themselves. It's hard to say what makes this realization happen and it's most likely different for each person. So, if you don't fit the high school or college scenario described below, don't worry. This book still applies. In fact, it may apply more since you're at a point when most of the ground work described here has clearly proven to be true from what you've experienced.

So, what's a life plan. How do you pick that point on the horizon you hope to achieve? Aahhh, we've hit on a subject practically never discussed. If you're like most people you drifted through high school with no particular direction. You either did well or were just happy to get enough credits to graduate. At that time in life usually the only "plan" anyone has is to finish school and get a job. Or, finish school and go to college...sometimes the college crowd goes so far as to include "I'm going to be a "fill in your own idea" when I graduate from college. On the other hand, they more often go off to college with a plan no deeper than to graduate. And, that leads us to answering the question of why so many college graduates can't find a job. In many cases they chose a field of study they liked, maybe because it was "easy". But, they never wondered how a career in that field would provide the goals of their life plan, usually because they had no life plan and gave planning their life no thought. You can't execute the steps to achieve your goal if you don't have a plan with a goal.

In either case there's no real grasp of what it's going to take to succeed at their "life" plan....because they don't have one. It's never been thought of or considered, at least not in enough detail to matter. At that point in life there's some vague idea about what a good life is but people really don't know what they want or what it takes to get there. The high school grad is thinking I'll get a job at "fill in the blank" and be able to do what I want. The college bound student figures I'll get a degree in "fill in the blank" and do the job(s) I want for the rest of my life.

The High School Graduate

So, we'll discuss the high school grad first. No one, including the graduate himself, has considered "what do I want to be doing in five or ten years". No one ever pointed out that a life starting from scratch, with no particular skill or life plan, is almost impossible to work out and make him/her happy. If it does it's either entirely luck or you just changed your goals to match what you got. In that case you've "settled" for what life gave you. You didn't reach your goal, you stopped at a goal someone else determined for you.

    If you get out of high school and go to one of the armed services, that can be a great choice. Not only does it give you structure, discipline and perspective but you begin to understand what makes the world go around. You see multiple types of conduct, multiple ways to handle authority and, in general, learn what you like and don't like as a lifestyle. The service can be a good lifestyle and suites a great number of people. For me, I don't see it as a career. What I observed was the difficulty associated with having a family and being absent for long periods of time. If you're single it's a great life full of adventure, good times and training. If you have a spouse and perhaps a family it's tough. At that young age a mind and body can wander which doesn't do anyone any good.

    Now, don't get me wrong, I'm not anti-marriage or family. I'm just saying before you get into that scenario think about what you're doing. If you haven't thought beyond the great time you're having….you're making a mistake. Is this the way I want to go through life? Is this the only person who can make you happy for all the years to come? Many times, the answer is NO. Fun times are just that FUN TIMES. Try to look ahead, see your horizon, be realistic and don't tie yourself to a situation that will almost certainly set you on the wrong course for the rest of your life. Try to think of what you want in life, what kind of "plan" you have or want to have. If you let the fun times rule and make decisions based strictly on having a good time, it's a mistake. You'll find later the price to pay for that decision is much more than you ever anticipated or wanted. And that's exactly why having thought things through and picking your point on the horizon can keep you out of trouble.

    Maybe the armed service wasn't for you; it wasn't a choice you felt you could consider. No problem, it's not for everyone. But you do need a job. It can and should be anything you can get. Obviously, it depends on what's open, what you can qualify to do and what meets your needs. Don't overlook the aspect of "who you know". I'd say more than half the time a job is secured in one way or another by who you know, who can give you the break to get hired that first time.

    At this point, with no skill and perhaps no contacts, you have to take what you can get. But you should take that first job with a plan. Does this job lead to a skill you can build on? Does this job have the option for moving up within the company? Can you make a career in this company that will meet your personal goals and get you to your point on the horizon? And THAT is the best question to ask yourself. How does this job fit into what I want my life to be like? It may not fit and you're doing it only until you qualify to move on. But, don't think that and have no plan for moving on. That would really just mean you have no plan and very likely will be stuck drifting through life settling for what it gives you. Bullshit………HAVE A PLAN AND EXECUTE IT. I'm in a dead-end job but I'm going to school at night to be a "whatever". Or, I'm in a dead-end job but I'm learning a skill or getting experience necessary to get my next job. And I'm making my move to my next job in a specific amount of time. Have a specific timeframe that suits the situation. Without thinking of WHEN the next step happens…..you don't have a next step.

    It's not necessarily a bad thing to graduate from high school and get a job. It doesn't mean you're going to be relegated to a lower standard of living for your lifetime. That may happen but only if you let it. If you have a goal then your start is as good as anyone else. And why? Because you're going to make it happen! You're going to work your plan until what you want does happen. You have your point on the horizon, you have an objective and you're not going to let anything stop you from reaching it. It does NOT mean your plan is flawless. It does not mean everything you plan is going to work just the way you want it to. NOT AT ALL. It means that when something happens to block your way, something changes and the path you intended to follow isn't working out……….YOU CHANGE YOUR PATH. But you do not change your point on the horizon. Sure, it may take longer than you wanted. Sure, it might mean you have to do things you didn't want to do. (you changed jobs five times instead of one or two). But you keep your eye on the end goal and make whatever changes necessary to get there. Keep in mind hard work, a good attitude, persistence and dedication to doing a good job always win. Every employer values these qualities. While that does not mean you'll be recognized quickly as the one to promote, it does mean you'll be recognized and gain the skills needed to advance. It's not always what you know. It's also how people perceive you, whether or not you get along with your fellow workers and do what it takes to get things done. The ability to execute and drive to the completion of a task is exceptional……..and always stands out.

Example? I knew a guy who got a job right out of high school at a movie rental store. He worked hard and was good at what he did. He was very good with customers and in two years was promoted to manager of the store. He was making pretty good money, according to his plan, and felt like things were on track. One day he got an email from his regional boss saying the chain was eliminating stores and his would be one of the ones to go. He was devastated. All his work, all his efforts were for nothing. NOT TRUE. What he had learned was he did have what it would take to be successful. He now knew he could and would succeed. He had proved it! He knew he had skills to make his life what he wanted it to be. He shopped around, interviewed with a few companies. But, couldn't find an opportunity he felt lead to the goals he had in mind. So, he didn't take any of the jobs that were offered. He decided to start his own company doing handy man repairs. He was fairly skillful and he was very confident that he had the necessary people skills. So, he did. He made a plan, started slowly and built his business into just what he wanted. He became his dream. Sure, there were setbacks, sure it wasn't easy. But he never took his eye off his goal, his point on the horizon and drove to it regardless of the hurdles that came before him.

    This is one of many examples of how to make your plan work. How to drive to your goals no matter what hurdle comes before you. What makes this approach easy is to have a goal, with appropriate milestones along the way to the point on the horizon you want to achieve. You have to be persistent and never give up. Don't think you can relax and fall into the "woe is me" attitude. That's for losers! When something blocks your way, suck it up, find a way around the block and keep going. Most important is always be the worker who solves problems. Don't take the path of turning everything over to the boss. If you can't proceed without his approval at least present the problem with a suggested solution. Don't just hang it on the boss to figure out. Every boss will recognize the worker who gets things done, makes decisions, resolves the problems and makes things happen. Don't drift through your job, be the leader.

Al Uhryniak

The College Graduate

Then there's the college graduate who says "Oh, look at me, I went to college and I'll get a good job when I get out". Ok, what job? How many people get hired in that field every year? How many people are coming out of college with the same degree? What are my realistic chances of getting that first job I've been planning on?

Sadly, some of these important questions are not asked or answered by college students while they have a chance to change their path. It doesn't necessarily mean you have to change your career path. But it does mean you have to know the answers to those questions and make the appropriate decisions. What does it take to reach your goal? What is involved in getting to your point on the horizon?

If the top 10 or even 50 percent of graduates in this field find the job they had planned to get…..How did they qualify? What attributes did they have? Is it entirely on GPA at school? If so, you better hit those books and be as high as necessary to ensure getting in the "hired" group. Notice I didn't say "as high as you can". That might not be enough. If only people with a GPA of at least 3.8 get hired….then work your butt off until you have at least the 3.8. If you're going to say the best you can do is 3.0 then you really don't want the job. You really don't have what it's going to take to secure a job in the field. Change your "life plan" to one that doesn't require what you cannot or will not do. You have to be realistic or you're actually planning to "settle" for whatever life feels like giving you. If it takes having a wide range of interests and being deep in summer intern experience....then get it. Learn to play an instrument, have hobbies, get summer jobs usable as a quality reference. DO NOT wait for graduation and then look for your job, loser. There's no component of achieving your goal in waiting to see what happens. You have no plan if you're waiting to figure out how you're going to pay your college loans until after you graduate. Life is hard.......no one is lining up to bail you out.

And, there's another course of action if your plans to get hired into that field don't work out. Take a lower level job in the field. You might feel over qualified and you actually might be. But you have to take the job and work your way up, so to speak. You'll have to prove yourself, prove you have what it takes to be what you couldn't get hired to be. It gives you a chance to achieve your goal without having started with the assets needed to get hired into the job right out of school. If your goal on the horizon is a particular job then this is an option to get you there. It's an example of going around the hurdle, changing your path to your goal without giving up your goal. The horizon is far away and a very bumpy, difficult road leads to it. Be prepared and determined.

There is no one in the country who owes you anything. It's on you! The sooner you grasp this, the sooner you can become what you want. Most people talk about how things could have been except for "fill in the excuse". There will always be plenty of excuses to pick from. And that's why most people "settle" for what life gave them. They didn't think things through and identify their goal. And, without a goal you can't have milestones to the goal. They had no plan, no thought, and did nothing to ensure what they wanted was going to happen.

Once college is over the fun and good times are over. It's on you now. No one is providing you anything anymore. You can't skip class, you can't wear old, somewhat dirty clothes and still get by. You can't hang around with "fun" people or "easy" people and still accomplish your goals. The spouse type person who was so much fun and comfort in college may not be part of your "LIFE" plan. Remember fun times are just "fun times". Your point on the horizon includes your family situation. You have to include that in your goals.

Think!!! Plan!!!! Committing to a partner is most likely your first and most important ADULT decision. Don't make it because you feel good or like having someone to be with. This is your LIFE. What do you want it to be like five, ten, or fifty years from now? Life is long and hard bucking the daily grind. And if you're not happy with the personal life you've created, your work life will never be what you want it to be or what it could be. And, if you hate your job and have no future in it what chance do you have of making a happy personal life?

So, it's safe to say I endorse all three paths: the armed services, college and starting right out of high school. Each of those choices present great opportunities as a choice of places to work and learn. But they'll only lead to the lifestyle you want if you've thought that through and it meets your needs. Have a goal. You need to decide what you want your life to be like, what will make you happy on the retirement home porch rocking in the rocking chair. Get that goal in mind and make all your decisions based on getting to that goal. And for God's sake EXECUTE the plan that gets you there.

Nugget: don't drift into or through your life. Have a plan. It can have options and several milestone points on the way, but don't just let things happen without knowing where you're pointed on the horizon. Your plan can be as simple as: I'm going to have a solid job that I like. A job with a future of more money and responsibility. A job that's secure so I can get married, raise a family and provide more opportunities for my children than I had when I started out. This doesn't mean you can't go out, can't date, can't have fun and toys like boats and cars. But, you'll have to look for a spouse and a lifestyle that will support those goals and a work plan that makes it happen. And that plan isn't a plan unless you have a timeline. A plan without a timeline isn't a plan; it's a wish that isn't going to come true. And a plan with a timeline that you ignore isn't a plan either. The endless pursuit of your goal for life and work…makes it happen. Do what it takes to get it done. If there are obstacles, remove them, hurdles, jump them or go around. And, if there are impossible barriers to your goal, change the path to get to your goal so the barrier doesn't matter. But don't stop and wait until the barrier goes away. That is not a plan; that's a tooth fairy who isn't coming.

Setting the Stage

Before we begin lets first explain the "point on the horizon" idea. This book assumes your point on the horizon isn't going to be achieved because you worked on the assembly line for forty years. Nay, Nay, it assumes your plans have to include owning or managing some group or company. It assumes you won't achieve your goals by being "in the workforce". It assumes your goals are higher, more aggressive and include a clearly exceptional point on the horizon. And while there should be and will be many milestone achievements along the way, it's trying to point out the "shot and beer" mentality that will make it happen.

After many years in life and business I see people managing their lives who are divided into two categories. One is a passive, politically correct person. This category of people will make decisions about their life or work but will take little or no action to execute a plan that makes it happen. Most of their life decisions are made by circumstances and not by them. That really is making no actual decision at all. When they make a work decision it's generally after considerable thought, possibly including countless meetings and a definite sense that they know the decision has a high probability of achieving the intended goal. While they don't have the confidence to act on what they think is the right course, at least they do what they think is necessary to gain that confidence. This part of their decision process leads to long delays and possible inaccurate influences, but at least a final decision is made. Many times, this decision comes too late to address the problem and they've lost not only the opportunity to correct it but they allowed employee attitude to deteriorate. However, this is where their plan falls apart. They have a decision but no interest or ability in doing what's necessary to create and execute a plan to make it happen. Perhaps the goal is so far away they can't break it down into manageable parts. Perhaps they get started but at the first sign of resistance they abandon the effort. But mostly it boils down to not being able to follow up and make sure the focus stays on the goal. If you want to get to your goal, this is the worst configuration of events possible.

    Just let me say that today the businesses of the United States and most likely the entire world are filled with passive managers. They are at every level of management and own or operate many companies. In every case their companies are less efficient than they could be and earn less every day than is actually possible. They are profitable but not at or maybe even not near their maximum performance level. And for examples just look at the steel industry, the automobile Industry or any large company you know of which isn't as profitable or prominent as it once was. What killed them? What did them in? Their inability to look ahead, create and execute a plan pure and simple.

The other group of managers, and by far the smaller group, are those who execute plans to reach their goals. This group is not smarter, more business savvy or blessed with the ability to see the future. No, these people are just a group who realizes what's best for their lives or their company is the best decision. They investigate options regardless of the perceived resistance and choose what seems best. They plan and look forward while having a plan to avoid downturns always protecting the stability and longevity of the company. This is the group of managers who create a growth company with satisfied employees and customers; a company where mistakes are made but not penalized because "if you're not making mistakes you're not doing your job as a manager". A company where employee ideas and input are valued. These people know that to achieve your goal you must be fair, decisive and hold to a set of rules and guidelines regardless of the popularity or resistance which may come from their decisions. But, most importantly, they execute their plans. Most importantly they follow through and either get the results they need or CHANGE the plan so they can get to the end point. If you think any plan by any person will be perfect YOU ARE WRONG. Plans require change. Plans require modification. But the goal isn't to create the perfect plan. The goal is to create the best plan you can and modify it as needed to get what you want. That is true in life and work. Don't forget the value of change, focus on your goal, the point on the horizon.

Because these people are decisive, they make mistakes. If they face 50 decisions a week, 40 will be good, 5 will be ok and 5 will turn out to be wrong. They see no problem with this and change their decisions to match situations when additional information is available or where what sounded good just doesn't work. They don't continue on with a bad decision just to avoid looking like they didn't know the right answer the first time.

Let me say here at the start that the size of the group does not matter. You are always managing yourself but you might also be managing one or two people who work alongside you. Or, you could be managing a crew of people who work together or independently to accomplish some specific task. You might also be managing one or more people (crew leaders, supervisors or managers) who in turn manage others. The important points you find in this book apply to all those situations. You'll have to modify the application of each point to suit the situation. But the fact remains constant in how each point will provide guidance and results in every situation. For the purpose of these points of guidance "size doesn't matter".

What's key, what's really important in your personal and work life is that you know where the point on the horizon is and where you stand on the road to get there. Don't deviate from your goal. Deviating on the path you're taking most certainly will occur. You have to adjust for situations, conditions and changes to your timeline. But the goal remains the same. You can't drive to a point on the horizon if it's not there.

Now speaking of your goal or your current point on the horizon does not mean you have to have your entire life figured out right off the bat. In fact, that would be nice but I'm sure it almost never happens. Most likely the best anyone can do is to know the next goal they want to achieve. So, what really happens is you have a series of points on the horizon. Achieving one doesn't mean you're done. It means you have attained a milestone on the way to your final goal. And you may not even know your final goal. All you might know is that when you get to your next goal you'll decide where you want to be after that. And that is also a great position to be in. Don't give any thought or worry to not knowing where you want to be after you reach your next goal or milestone. It's not a bad thing to decide what that is by doing it one goal at a time. Just be aware of all the danger in "settling". If you decide you've reached your final goal that's fine. But the danger is deciding where you're at is your final goal because going on is too hard, complicated or challenging. Being a settler in an old western movie is fine. Being someone who settles in life is not fine; it's giving up.

Ok, you spent the money and bought the book. Now you wonder "what am I going to get?" When are these nuggets of wisdom going to start appearing? Well, pay attention, here they come.

Just remember this point: Everyone is ABLE to be successful, but very few people are WILLING to do what it takes to be successful.

Your First Job

Like almost every person who ever joined the workforce you have to find that first job. Sometimes it's while you're in school, high school or college, and sometimes it's after you graduate. It really doesn't matter; the same approach is what you should use in either case.

The "boss" whether you work for the owner or just your group boss, wants the worker who is congenial, can keep things moving, doesn't complain and in general gets everything done that needs to be done. And, the worker should do this without complaining, whining or needing continuous guidance. They just make it happen. So, what does that mean? How does this apply to the jobs that are normally considered "entry level" or even part time or temporary. Lets' consider a couple specifics but remember your attitude is everything.

The part time worker in a movie theater. Some days he works as a ticket taker, sometimes he might be behind the snack counter and sometimes he might be in the booth out front selling tickets. Whatever the assignment you need to follow the guidelines we mentioned above. And to do that you have to have the right approach.

Understand what needs to be done. Each job assignment has specific rules or tasks that can't be skipped or overlooked. Make sure you know them. When deviations occur take care of them to satisfy the customer as long as the resolution isn't going to break one of the rules of that specific job. As you gain experience you'll find out what the boss will do in each case where an odd thing happens. Use this information to guide you when it happens the next time. If you know what the boss does to resolve the problem you MAY be able to do that the next time without getting him involved. MOST times the boss is going to appreciate a satisfied customer who was treated just the way he would have done it if he were called to make the resolution. And, most importantly, the customer is going to appreciate a resolution that was handled quickly without having to wait for "the boss" to get there to make the decision. I've emphasized the MAY and MOST because you will find bosses who don't want you to resolve problems. You will find bosses who don't want you to make decisions. Usually this is because they want to be the "boss" and show people decisions have to come to them. But, once you learn that you can act accordingly while still being impressive.

In a different job position your customer will be someone else in the business. You're doing work that prepares or creates something that's used by another employee. They're still YOUR customer. Do what's best for them. Find out what they need, see if doing a little more or doing the preparation another way would be better for them. You want to make your customer happy. You want them to endorse your work and mention they really like when you're working because it's easier or quicker for them when you're doing their prep. And, most of all, make every attempt to display a positive, helpful, "I can do more" attitude all the time. Attitude is infectious and it makes those around you feel better. It's just the icing on the cake to make that "customer" or your fellow workers feel good about you being in your job.

You'll want to not only learn the job you're in but learn the operation. It might be that there are other positions at this company which aren't entry level spots. If that's true you want to position yourself to either be promoted or to be able to come back later and apply for another job. You want to be able to use your first round of employment there as the key to getting that job. And above all, you want to use this job to rely on for a recommendation for any next job. It's not just the time you invested here to get the money you needed. That's surely one thing but NOT the main thing. You've spent the time working there and you definitely want it to count as a recommendation for the NEXT job.

So, in a case like this, what's your plan and in what way does acting like this help your plan get accomplished? It's simple! Your plan is multi-pointed. On one hand you're developing the skill you'll use your entire working life. You're developing a style for executing the job. No one likes being in a good mood and pleasant every day. It's tough. Some days you're not in a good mood. Some days you don't feel like being nice or helping anyone.

That's why it's hard. Put aside your feelings for a few hours and make things happen in the right way. After all, you have to be there anyway; what's the advantage of making sure everyone knows you're having a bad day…..there isn't any. You don't want to create the impression that you're usually a good worker but some days you're no better than the worst guy. That create the impression you're just "putting in on" when you're the good guy.

Another impression you're creating is that you're able to handle more than what you've been given. You want to be the first name to come up when an opening, promotion or job option comes up. While you're not going to be in the discussion you want someone who is to say "What about Herman? He's a hell of a worker and a really nice guy. We should see if he wants this move". It may not fit your plan so you may not take it; you may not even like the idea of it. But, you want to be thought of as the first choice for the offer. USUALLY, if you turn it down with a good reason it doesn't do any harm and you can still be in line for the next opening.

And at this point what's your plan? You should have a couple objectives. First you are developing the skill and style you're going to use in every job from now on. It's not easy and as the years go by you'll constantly be relearning how to deal with personalities and attitudes of co-workers and bosses. Just remember most of the people in the business world are passive managers. You'll be dealing with them and their management weaknesses all your life.

This might be a good time to talk about the passive manager. You have to realize this group is not without a purpose. They are smart people and do have good ideas. While you want to understand their value you also must recognize their inherent weakness. They cannot execute a plan or a change. They can think of it, identify some of the necessary steps to implement it and even start the process. But they cannot carry it through. And, most of what they do to get the new plan or change started is either wrong, weak or poorly thought through. Couple all of this with their inability to eliminate hurdles faced by making a change and their lack of skill or desire to modify their implementation strategy. So, for the most part this is why they usually fail at change.

But their weakness or soft management style is your best friend. You can be easily recognized as an asset by applying your "shot and beer" attitude and your ability to get things done when a plan for change is being developed or implemented. Be the one who sees each hurdle as an opportunity. Be the one who makes suggestions about how to modify the plan, eliminate the hurdle and get the change accomplished. In these situations, you'll find your time to shine without doing any more than focusing on the goal, making any necessary changes to the plan and getting things done. In short you'll apply your Shot and Beer attitude to the execution of the plan and make it successful.

The One Man Show

For whatever reason you've been forced to join the real world and make your own way. Perhaps you just got out of the service and don't want to work for someone else. Or perhaps you just graduated (college or high school) and feel your best choice for making it is to be your own boss. It might even be that after a few years working for someone you've decided you want to live or die on your own mistakes and not those made by someone else. It doesn't matter what the reason might be, you can do this if you're careful. Having a trade or a craft is a great, solid position to be in. Or, if you find yourself with the stomach to buy a small existing business which may not be doing so well maybe that's your choice. But buying a "failing" business might be your best choice after you've gotten comfortable with achieving goals along the path of a plan. It's probably not a great first choice. And, there are several business ventures you can get into that don't take much skill or knowledge to begin.

Perhaps you can work on cars and that seems like a good business to start? Maybe plumbing or electrical work is a field you have knowledge of? Most likely you'll have no practical experience but still want to work for yourself. So, say, as an example, you've decided to start a lawn care business. It seems an easy way to begin. There isn't much equipment involved, the overhead is low and the skill level required seems easy enough to achieve.

So, perhaps along with support from your spouse, you figure you can mow grass all day, every day, driving around in your own vehicle and be just fine. You think; there's no one to bother me, no one to tell me what to do and the money I get each month from my customers will be plenty for us to live on. But, what kind of plan do you have to put together to make this great idea work?

And you figure, first I'm going to need to know what my expenses are going to be. I'll need a vehicle to drive and maybe a trailer to haul my equipment. And of course, there's the equipment itself. Maybe I can start by using a pickup and carry everything in the bed to avoid the trailer? There's gas for the truck & the equipment. There's upkeep for maintaining everything in good working condition. Ok, I'm ready............NOT.

You skipped "a couple" steps. You don't know anything about the business of cutting grass. How much do companies in the business charge to cut grass? How many yards can I cut in a day, every day? How much do I have to charge to make a profit? This is the basic calculation every manager has to make to understand how to manage their area of responsibility. This is "force & load" balancing. Force is defined as what resources it takes to do the work and what does that cost balanced against Load; how much product can be produced and what revenue do you get from it. No matter what your job is, in management, you'll never get away from this basic question of force & load.

For this example, you determine that 100 customers a month (20/day each week) is what you can cut. At 100 customers you'll have the income you'll need to pay expenses and make a profit. You also realize you'll need a helper or partner who trims and blows while you do the cutting. All you need is the 100 customers and you're in a profitable business. And you march out to knock on doors to talk 100 people into using you to care for their lawn.

Lets' think about just how you're going to crack into this market. What about appearance? When you approach a lawn care prospect, that first impression is critical. You are the company. You have to present yourself in a way that makes that particular customer comfortable.

Sure, you like tattoos. That one of your ex-girlfriend is nice. And sure, having one or more doesn't make you a bad guy. It doesn't make you any less knowledgeable about lawn types and how, when and why to care for them. But, as you walk up the walk the customer has already judged you and decided he doesn't want you lurking about his house. Is it fair? No. But it's reality and everything affecting your success has to be taken into consideration. Take the time to think through every aspect of what you're providing. In the case of a lawn care business its price, appearance, quality, reliability, and attitude....basically the comfort of knowing that in every way the customers "like" you and what you do. They "like" their neighbors making positive comments about not only their lawn but the people who take care of it. What the customer hears his neighbors saying is "you must be really smart to have selected a great company like that".

So, you have a great smile, you speak well and tell a story about doing the best job ever on the lawns. You've put on long sleeve shirts to get around the whole "tattoo" thing. And you keep every promise you've made to the customers. Occasionally you go back at the end of a day to resolve a complaint from a customer who wasn't really right but why not just make them feel better. You're mowing on weekdays and calling on potential customers at night and weekends.

At first you just have fifteen customers but before long you get to 50 and start using the second guy to help out each day. You're developing a good reputation and your customer base is growing. You're having fun at work, things are going "ok" and you know you'll be able to reach the 100-customer level you felt would be exactly where you wanted to be. Life is good.

You assume that to be the best lawn care company you just need to be doing the best job ever. You never took the time to think about what it takes to be considered "the best". Any bumbler who can walk and chew gum can cut grass. You bought this book to be the best that ever was. Great service is what will make your customers happy and pass your name along to others who can become new customers. There are a million lawn care companies and almost all of them make ends meet.....but few are exceptional and have owners who spend their winters in Florida at their winter home.

Planning and execution my friend, this is what separates the great managers from the rest. What are you going to do when it rains and you lose a day mowing? What do you pay the helper for down time? If you don't pay him will he come back tomorrow? What will you do when grass isn't growing in the cold months?

Have you figured insurance into your equation? You certainly don't want to be exposed to lawsuits when something goes wrong, in or out of your control. What about paying your Workman Compensation insurance? Was that figured into the budget? When you hired your helper did you do that thinking of when you added another crew he would lead that crew? Was your plan to have him teach and monitor quality for his new guy while you did the same with your new helper? No, most likely you never got there in your plan. You never considered what capacity your spouse had for doing the billing. And, you never took into account how to hold good, trained workers through the off season so you'd have them next year.

  You have your spouse doing the billing and doing a really good job at 50 customers. But the job is getting more time consuming by the week and occasionally a mistake is made. Not a big one, but still a mistake. Maybe the bill is late, maybe a check isn't cashed on time, maybe a little extra for trimming a shrub or spreading mulch isn't shown in the correct billing cycle. It's a crack in the dyke, a small thing but customers begin to wonder "is he getting too big"?

  At the same time the 100-customer goal has been passed and you're now stretched at 120 customers. You really don't have the time or energy to call on prospects at night or weekends. Some equipment maintenance has been skipped and occasionally causes problems during the day. Still, you're holding it together and keeping everyone happy.

But, all of this is because you never planned for reaching your goal. You were so focused on getting the 100 customers you never thought about what to do when you got there, when winter came or when you needed another crew. In short you built your business to be one size....and then you were too successful and too short sighted at the same time.

What was your goal? Was it getting to 100 customers? If so, why? That wasn't going to get you to your point on the horizon. That wasn't going to be where you wanted to end your career. You picked a good milestone, a good goal for your first achievement but it was just a part of the path to get you to your final goal. Your horizon goal is the end point. You may and should have several intermediate goals along the path. But, don't confuse them with your end point. If you've thought things through, if you really have developed a plan, your point on the horizon is going to guide you all along the way.

You're not a helper, a worker, a floater or an employee………..you are managing the business! You are the owner! But you didn't have a plan for "what if". And if you don't have a plan you certainly can't execute it.

Being in charge of or owning any business is a good thing. It's fun, exciting, exhausting and frustrating with huge risks and rewards. But, if you're not prepared, if you didn't think about what it really takes to manage it, then you've failed before you started. Planning and execution are crucial…….but not easy. It's one big reason there are a great many passive managers and very few people who can do what's necessary to reach a goal.

I'm sure there are points to consider for your lawn care business not listed here. But, I'm not really giving you a roadmap for starting a lawn care business. What I'm trying to make you realize is how to look at what you want to do and prepare yourself. It doesn't matter what business you have an interest in starting. I want you to know from the very start how critical it is to plan. From the guy who runs a one-man business to the corporate mogul, everyone has to have a plan and execute that plan; you have to keep revising it and updating it to align with your "point on the horizon". Without that, you're lost.

Your Management Responsibility

So, based on what you've read so far, what is the first thing you need to do? Your first task has to be determining "what product or service does my group produce?" In this scenario "product" means what is this group supposed to accomplish and "group" may also mean company. This might be a service, an actual product or some task or set of tasks which set up some other group to do their work. It doesn't matter. Your first concern is to know the what, where, when, how and why for the "product" your group is responsible to deliver. This is basic research information you need to know since all your decisions will be based on what you've determined at this point. As time goes by some of these reasons will change as the market changes but you have to start with how it is today.

Now, you've decided how the group's "product" affects others. And you know this because you carefully thought it through and investigated the situation based on what the group produces. But, here's a caution you have to address prior to beginning. You have to decide what YOU are supposed to do. What will be the measurement of YOUR success? Many times, people start off without a clear understanding of just what results will be considered good. And if you don't know that, you not only have trouble meeting the goal, you almost assuredly can't exceed it. So, you can just ask yourself, "What do I have to do to be the best at this?" Because you bought this book to be someone who can execute a plan that means you want to be results oriented. Anyone who stumbles down the street can manage a group but you bought the book to not only be the best at it but to be clearly the best.

    This is by far the most dangerous part of your beginning. Don't allow yourself to be caught up doing what's obvious or what was always done. If you ever hear the phrase similar to "we always did it like this" you can bet the farm there are changes which should be made. Nothing stays the same and when any group thinks what's being done is the best way to do it…they're wrong.

    While managing any size group you can choose to ignore any or all of the aspects of how customers grade you. But each area where the customer grades you need to be an A+ if you want to be successful. So, what does that take? Think the job through. What service or product do you provide and why would someone like getting it from you so much they recommend you to others. Why would other work groups easily recognize what your group does as so much better than before? Why would they go out of their way to talk about your management skill? The answer is because you understand what they want. As I said, the size of the group and the product you produce doesn't matter. All of the preparation is the same if you're going to achieve a recognizably better product and not just be average. Every Tom, Dick and Henry can be average......and average doesn't win.

Example. If you're in a situation where you're going to be in charge of some people (remember size doesn't matter) the same point applies. First you have to decide what results will make you outstanding. Most times, if you have a boss, he doesn't know any more than you do about answering that question. If asked, he immediately starts some long-winded explanation, while sounding slightly annoyed, about what you should be doing. And, generally he/she will attempt to leave you feeling inadequate for even asking. As an example, you might be put in charge of people who have been doing their particular jobs for quite a while. And the boss might be annoyed by your question because what he expects of you is to keep things going just as they are. In effect, he doesn't want a supervisor or manager, he wants a clerk to answer questions and make sure the people show up and report their time correctly. But what he says to you covers up what he's thinking which is most likely "Good Grief, if you don't know how you're going to manage this group maybe I picked the wrong guy".

Most times they hope they leave you feeling insecure with an attitude that you should keep quiet and make sure nothing changes or needs to be passed up the chain above you. Sometimes they won't know enough about the position to give you any insight but they'll hide that detail. Now, before you get all sweaty and start thinking of all the ways to make sure the boss knows how important you're going to be....stop and consider what you should be doing.

Get as little detailed "guidance" information about the job you have to do as is possible. The less you are told about what specifically to do and how to do it, the better. If you get specific instructions it only limits your ability to think the job through. And when you achieve some new results from changes you made it puts you in a position to get the response "I/we told you what the job was and it wasn't that". In this case you have to explain why you did what you did when all you really want to talk about is what the results of that action are. This is a tactic almost every passive manager will use to squash innovation and change. You get so caught up in explaining the "WHY your investigating making changes" that days or weeks are spent defending your position. And, it's very likely you'll be told to stop.

Give the boss updates about work as it flows through your group. Mention where you think things bottleneck and how the change you made resolved it. Don't bring up a problem without talking about what you did to resolve it. You're taking action not being a passive butt kisser. Remember what I said earlier, most management people just watch, they don't manage. These people are afraid of change and afraid of anything that might rock the boat. Changing processes, even when it will bring obvious improvement, is usually resisted by those above and below. Change brings questions which does not create a comfortable situation. Passive managers will avoid it.

Your action item here is "think". Don't allow yourself to overlook questioning the details of how something is being done "because it's already obviously the right way". It might be, but it also might not be the right way anymore.

Things change and as they do the way they're handled should also change. Look at your job as an Innovator. Regardless of how long it's been done or how smoothly it appears to work, is it still the best way to do it? It may not need to be done at all? In the example of lawn care, you could easily say "show up on time each week, do a great job cutting, trimming and blowing the clippings and leave the lawn looking good." It's a perfectly reasonable conclusion and most every lawn care company would be very happy with that result after each visit. But consider the customers point of view and points he might be thinking. "The boss never comes to the door when they arrive just to let me know they're here, he never tells me when they're done. He doesn't ask if he can get water from the hose, he just does it. His bills are late, incomplete or wrong as the seasons change and specialty work is done. Sometimes my check gets cashed the same day I pay him and other times it might be the next week. I'm not sure he's treating this like a real business. I just don't feel like he respects me or understands that I'm his customer".

As the manager you have to think about every angle of the job. It's not enough to produce a great product, you have to also do it so well the customer sees the difference. In the lawn care example, it's easy to walk through the steps you need to take. You want to be impressive and have a process that addresses customer concerns before he brings them up to you.

If you're working with a group and your customer is another group in the same company the steps you need to take are more difficult to uncover. But, the objective is the same. Find out what they need from your group, find out the when, why and how your piece works best for them. Then deliver it in such a way as to clearly identify your group, and therefore yourself, as going above and beyond their expectations.

And don't stop by focusing on your product. Make sure you look at what product or information you get to start with. Do whatever can be done to make the chain of delivery to you as simple for the down-stream group as possible. Always remember you want the end to end process to be better not just your obvious portion. The more you know about the end to end flow of work the easier it is to manage effectively.

Example: I worked in a large company where my group took information passed to us as an order, prepared it for delivery and passed it to the delivery group. For several years before I arrived there developed a running battle with the order creation group to provide all the information we needed to handle the order. For years there were meetings, notices, arguments and people on both sides getting rated poorly based of how orders were written in the most recent measurement period. When I looked into this "problem" I was told how critical it was and that the other group would never do their part well enough....so I better watch them like a

The Shot and Beer Manager

hawk. As a new manager I clearly made this my top priority and jumped on the problem. But what I found was the information, most often in question, was wrong more than half the time because the source the first group had was, would never, and could never be accurate. To that end my group, as part of their process, always verified the information themselves. And, because our source for the information was completely accurate and easy to use, it took only minutes, and was never wrong. But, because the process which had been in place for years, said we should get a flawless order address as the order came in, we spent hours and sometimes days waiting for a verification or reissue of the order. All of this because the existing process dictated the address was supposed to be there and be completely accurate when we received the order.

After investigation and on my own, I changed the process. I had my people continue to look up every address but without the verification step to see if the one that existed on the order was 100% accurate. The error rate immediately went to practically zero. On-time delivery percentages jumped to practically 100 percent. I was an immediate sensation for doing nothing more than looking into the problem to see if it could be fixed. For years before me, every manager of my group had beaten the drum for the order taking group to do their job. No one ever considered whether or not the job actually needed to be done. Even if this change would have added time to my part of the process, it would have been a change for the better. Its implementation produced tremendous savings for the order creation group, added no extra time to my group and made orders available to the delivery group in time to make the originally promised due date. This is management reacting to a situation and making changes at its best.

Ok, now you've decided what your responsibility is in your position. But that doesn't mean you're going to be successful. You still don't have a plan. And, my friend, the plan is critical. It's not critical enough to be the first thing you decide. But, you have to have a plan that matches what you're going to do. It's the part that defines the necessities that have to be in place to make it happen.

I have heard the comment made that "oh, the business failed because they were too successful." That actually means the manager had defined his role in the business but never created a plan. Almost every case where this failure occurs there was also no "flexibility" in the manager to adjust and make things work. This scenario creates a situation where decisions were made and kept in place long after they could have possibly worked. In fact, the company was doomed long before it ever closed its doors.

So, you say, just what is the "planning" you talk about. If the manager knew what his role was and was paying attention to those responsibilities how could he fail. It's easy, he never considered how the work flowed through his pipe. How each job or task actually entered the process and flowed to completion, what it took to complete it, how much was going to be completed, by whom, doing what and all being done with the quality level needed to be successful. It's That Simple!!!!

The Shot and Beer Manager

Lets' say we're in the lawn care example. The manager is doing everything he thought about prior to starting. He's covered the solicitation of new customer's angle, he's got a helper who knows exactly what to do, and he's with him all day ensuring quality. And, he has made him very aware of how to act and talk whenever a customer or potential customer can hear or see him. Everything is going perfectly and according to plan. They keep adding customers until one crew just can't keep up. It's time to add another crew and he puts his helper in charge of the second crew and hires two new helpers, one for him and one for the second crew. it's a great day for the business.

He knows the man he put in charge of the new crew has the skills and knowledge to do exactly what is right and makes customers happy. He checks with him every night to make sure all the work was completed and things are going well. But, he's not there. He hears what is said but he doesn't know if it's true or if it means the same as if he were saying it. While the new crew leader was a great helper, does he really have the qualities to run his own crew? Is he capable of leading so that customer care and job quality remain the same? Is the equipment being kept up as it was before? Are the rules being followed or did the crew slack off? Is the same level of quality being delivered? What's the quality control aspect of this expansion?

Soon he starts hearing complaints. Just little ones at first but they are the sign things have gone wrong. Before long he has to take time in the evening to check with complaining customers. The actual results of what he thought was a good plan are not acceptable. Ok, make whatever changes are necessary to correct it, in short, make a new plan. But do something. Continuously telling the new crew leader to do better is not a plan. What saved his company and positioned him to grow was his new plan. After much thought he realized that to grow he could not be a crew leader himself. He needed to be the boss, responsible for quality and customer satisfaction while adding new customers to grow the business. He not only created two crews but started adding customers to grow to three crews. He realized his plan was in error. He didn't have any way of actually managing what was done by being one of the crew leaders himself. But, by being the boss, having the time to monitor and enforce his quality standards, he was able to add customers while ensuring quality, satisfaction and growth. And all of this could be done while earning enough to pay himself for being in the boss role. This is a clear example of how you change the plan to get yourself back on track and reach your goal. While the original plan sounded good it didn't work as a day to day operation. There was no way to guarantee quality, satisfy customers and grow the business with the first plan.

    In a larger company it can be even worse. You may be in charge of one group working with other groups to get things done. Your group is part of the flow the product follows as it moves through the pipe to delivery. The company is successful at sales and orders are coming in just as planned. But the process being followed by the groups involved in producing the product are not keeping up. At first the normal, and often appropriate, reaction is to add people. Reinforce the processes so that more work can be completed at each spot where things seem to slow down. This is a sign, an indicator, that you need to revisit your processes and ensure things are flowing in the most effective way.

In the planning stages, each manager has to decide the capacity level for work in his group. I might realize that my group finishes 50 tasks a day and passes them on ready for the next group. I see the steps involved in the completion and have enough people to increase to 60 tasks a day if needed. But, what about 70, or more? What do I do then? Well, unless I get more people or change the way I do the tasks I'll have to rely on overtime. Generally, the remedies are added in the same order with overtime for the occasional peak used as the first choice. Additional people are added when the workload is determined to have increased permanently. I'm not overlooking "part-time" help which has its own complexity and shortcomings. It can be a viable option if used correctly for temporary, longer term changes.

Now, here is where the shot and beer manager who gets things done, is separated from the passive manager. When the manager who plans and executes is faced with this situation he looks at what it's going to take to maintain the workflow requirement of on-time completion while increasing the output. The passive manager thinks of all the reasons the output level requirement needs to be adjusted to meet his work groups achievable output. While this seems subtle, the two situations couldn't be more different. One is a planned growth strategy, the other keeps the passive manager within his comfort zone, taking no risk. The manager who can execute a plan has or develops one that is focused on changes that gain efficiency and increases the output. The passive manager asks for more people, longer timelines or both while maintaining the same process flow that was in effect when the problem occurred.

As the manager who can plan and execute you have to look at what's best for the company. What was the long-range plan? They look for efficiency options BEFORE the need occurs. These managers are always aware of choices they might have to increase productivity without just adding people. This requires options for process change. And it's the very option passive managers avoid. Managers who can plan and execute look for a solution to put in place to accommodate conditions as they change in the next 18 months. Depending on the type of business and complexity of training or software enhancements it could be a longer period. A passive manager will always respond with a request for more people, longer time intervals or both. And make no mistake they are very good at laying out a case to justify their position. They've been doing it their entire career.

A passive manager likes to rely on charts, graphs and a process matrix to display what appears to be all the reasons the problem exists and that the only remedy is more people and longer timelines. He may also point out in a not so subtle way how other groups, certainly not his, are adding to the problem. This is a passive manager tactic and while good information can come from this prolific set of data, it must be viewed very cautiously.

The Small Business Operation

So, here you sit in a small business. You're the owner or the person in charge of running the day to day operation. It's your job to make sure everything works well and the business makes money. It doesn't matter how you got here. You might be the one who started the business, maybe you just bought a business that happened to be for sale and seemed like a good opportunity or maybe you've been hired to do the job. More likely you worked for the company for some time and finally got the break you wanted. Now is your time to shine and prove your worth. Actually, the nuggets you find here work in any of these scenarios so not to worry grasshopper.

Again, here is the basic calculation every manager has to make to understand how to manage the area they're responsible for: "force & load" balancing. Force is being defined as what resources and material it takes to do the work and what does that cost balanced against how much product can be produced and what revenue you get from it. This is generally called "return on investment" or ROI but knowing the correct term means nothing if you can't or don't do it. You have to understand your costs in time and money if you're going to have any chance at being profitable. No matter what your job is, in management, you'll never get away from this basic question.

I'm repeating this Force & Load balance information because it's always true. If you miss this, if you lose site of the big picture and allow yourself to get caught up in the million issues you'll tend to face each day, then you'll have a very tough time doing your job.

First figure out what the product is and what it takes to make it the best it can possibly be. Once you have that clearly in your mind you need to answer the second question which is "what return on the product do I need to be successful?" I hope you can see from this position what you're really doing. You're determining how much it costs to make your stuff (cost of the material, people and overhead) balanced against the money (revenue) you can get for your stuff (the product). Generally, what that means is just how much (the number of sold stuff) does it take to be profitable. You might be meeting every goal you set but if you based profitability on 1000 pieces of stuff and you're selling 800 you my friend are failing. It doesn't matter if the 800 pieces are the best ever…..you aren't going to be in business very long.

When you're small, running an operation that you oversee directly, you have to know what the people are doing. That does NOT mean you have to be able to do what they do. It means you need to look at what they do, how they do it, why they do it and think about what works well and what does not. For instance, you don't have to know how to operate and maintain the machine to cut lunchmeat for customers. But you better well know if the tasks they perform to operate, maintain and cut lunchmeat are logical, need to be done, are in the right order and can be improved. Why do you think every deli today precuts their lunchmeat and has it ready in the cold-case? It's because it just took too much time to cut it individually for each customer when they asked for it. The deli figured out what would be the "hot sellers" for the day. Then they had someone precut the lunchmeat so it took as little time as possible to serve each customer. That meant instead of using 5 minutes to get each customers baloney, it took 1 minute......and that's more baloney in a day......which equals more money generated by the same worker. Of course, some customers want their baloney cut fresh. That's a good thing because you do it with a smile. And while you're doing it the next guy in line is deciding to just take his from the already cut baloney because he's not waiting in line any longer. The end result is both customers are happy with the result and you sold more baloney in less time.

    In a small business it's relatively easy to know enough about the flow of work to make adjustments. But it doesn't happen automatically. I suggest you don't get caught up holding company meetings. Don't be creating company Mission Statements just because everyone has one. That's pointless! Most Mission Statements hang on a wall and after a couple weeks no one in the company can tell you what that Mission Statement is or means. It is by far better to LIVE the mission of the company...from top to bottom. That makes sense. Spending countless hours meeting to invent it, having it printed and framed and prominently displayed means nothing. Live the company mission. Make sure everyone knows it because they live it every day. Then, and only then, does it actually mean something.

Example. There was a division of a company whose director was very proud to be in charge and have a solid, well formed, mission statement. It was prominently displayed in several places throughout the buildings his groups used to do their work. During an Operational Review many of the employees were interviewed about how, why, when and where they did their jobs and what could make things better. NOT ONE of the employees mentioned or even knew the list of "guiding principles" the division director was so proud of. When the findings of the review were presented the director was stunned to hear no employee knew the mission. No employee had any of its guidelines incorporated into their daily work routine. Not only was the division failing but the director had surrounded himself with managers who told him what he wanted to hear. But, they had done nothing about implementing the guidelines of the mission statement. Shortly afterwards the director was replaced. He had done some good groundwork. Actually, he had a well-developed mission statement with guidelines that would have produced an effective workforce with an efficient workflow. But there was NO EXECUTION. The most important part was never put in place. While many of the managers participated in the failed operation of this division, the director was responsible.

Nugget: People (employees at any level) have good intentions (usually) and want to do a good job. But, if you don't check on them, if you don't make sure what you're being told is actually happening, IT'S NOT GOING TO HAPPEN!!! People are smart and if they sense you don't care (because you're not checking up) they stop doing that function.

Nugget: Workers know their shit….they know what will make things better. These are the people who do the job. The manager who can execute is very comfortable saying: "hey, how can we do this better? or what don't you like or what holds you up?" The employees know! Don't be stupid, just ask them. Passive managers never ask because they have a need to feel important. They have a pre-disposition to be "in-charge" at all times. They'd rather pass up a point of efficiency than admit they don't know what's best in every situation. And, even worse, actually much worse, is the passive manager who hears a suggestion and takes no action. Who would do that you ask……it happens every day at almost every company in the country. And why does it happen? I've been all over the country at companies in every state and always find managers are reluctant to make changes. They need multiple opinion sources all delivering the same message before they'll consider taking on the challenge of process change.

Nugget: workers give you what you want. Once you demonstrate you don't want or need their help……they stop helping! Oh, my goodness, could that be true? I'll bet almost everyone reading this book can think of a suggestion either they made or someone they know made and nothing was done. The worst thing possible any management person can do is "nothing".

Nugget: when you hear a suggestion do something. A high percentage of suggestions will fall into a category where they cannot be implemented. For a wide variety of reasons, it just isn't going to happen. Not because you didn't think of it but because it's not going to be done. You might want to and you might like to but you decided you're not going to do it. Example: An employee points out that Felix over there is only working at half speed and you should get rid of him. Well, you look into it and it's true. But, Felix was a good worker, has come on hard times, health or family issues, and you've decided to stick with him. That's a decision you made. It's not a bad decision…..it's what you've decided after understanding the issues. You know what's at stake and for reasons you feel are important, you made your decision.

Nugget: let people know. Sounds easy but it's the hardest part of doing what's right. It's actually the part of every suggestion most commonly overlooked. It is by far the core reason for dissention, poor performance and a bad attitude spreading throughout your business. The employees' opinion is: "I told him the problem and he did nothing about it" or "He can't say he doesn't know the problem; he's just not going to do anything about it". To the employee this means you arbitrarily decided to ignore an unfair situation. Employees will also create multiple

The Shot and Beer Manager

explanations for your inaction, none of them favorable to you. This gossip will grow and fester within the workers and adversely affect productivity. Poor workers will become even worst and good workers will deteriorate over time. And why? It's the working condition perception you created.

The passive manager can't do anything about this. They fear talking to employees about anything they have to defend. They don't have the stomach or confidence to back up their decisions directly to the employee. Somehow, they feel threatened having to explain their position, provided they even have one. Since their normal response to any suggestion is to ignore it, they never want to respond and explain or take a position.

Nugget: Be fair!! You're not inviting your employees over for dinner and a drink after work. You may not even like them personally. That's ok. They have a job and you do too. You pay them a reasonable wage and they perform their assignment. But, above all, you have to respect them and treat them fairly. In the example above that would mean going back to the person who brought up the issue. Take him aside and explain what you're going to do or not do and why. He definitely doesn't have to agree with your decision. Don't be caught up thinking you have to convince him or get his approval. The decision was and is yours. You made it, here's why and it's over. Many times, it will not be the answer he wanted to hear. But, you've stopped or mitigated most of the damage which can come from the issue by respecting the employee enough to give him an answer. AND, this is very important, do it in a timely manner, directly with whomever brought it up, in private. This is not a show or a test of will. You're the boss and here's what's going to happen....the end.

The best compliment an employee can pay his superior is to say "he's fair; not he's a nice guy or I really like him". Those opinions don't mean anything but will foster an environment where workers feel favoritism does or can exist. What you should strive for is a universal opinion that you're "fair" with everyone whenever you have to make a decision.

You might have noticed I never mentioned treating people equally. That's not necessary. What is necessary is making sure the way you treat people isn't arbitrary. If you're making decisions with values around who you "like" or who's the "best worker", you're also creating problems for yourself. And, you're avoiding the management role of dealing with the problem. If you have a "best worker" that really means you also have at least one "poor worker". That should be addressed to bring him up to standard. Don't just deal with the poor worker by avoiding the situation......deal with it. Have a discussion, explain your position. Have a list of reasons why this employee needs to step up. Have a plan for him to get to where he needs to be. Don't keep walking around the problem. Managers who can execute a plan deal with it, get it resolved and move on. If that means your brother-in-law has to be fired, then fire him.

Now please, don't take all my comments here to mean you should be getting rid of anyone who doesn't perform to your standards. One, it's against the law to discipline employees without just cause. And two, it's not treating people fairly and with respect. But you do have to have a plan. What is it going to take to get this person on track? Obviously, you considered him a good candidate at one time. Clearly, you've invested time and money training him. If he's not able or willing to meet those goals it's your responsibility to find out why and correct it. But, if after dealing with the employee honestly and providing him the opportunity to correct his situation, he doesn't show the progress you both committed to…….then take action. Don't shy away because it's distasteful. Don't continue to give the "one more chance" response just to avoid doing what you don't want to do. Have a plan, communicate the plan, execute the plan whether you like it or not. Keeping the poor performer in the company is a major error commonly made throughout businesses.

This doesn't always mean you have to fire him. Perhaps there are other jobs at the company you both feel would be a good fit. That's certainly a good direction to go. During your discussions you can explore that type of option to see if it makes sense. Remember, be honest, fair and respectful but execute.

So, management turns out to be hard work. Besides having to deal with all the decisions around force and load, you have these employee issues where you need to treat people fairly and with respect. Well, yes, that's what you need to do; but from that you get all the insight you could possibly hope for about running the business. No book, no research and no experience are going to be all you need to start or run a business. Even if your information was good at one time it most likely isn't as good today. In business everything changes. Your employees, products, public opinion, trends and the competition are never a static condition. Your job is to constantly be aware and adjust. I think I've mentioned planning.........it all comes down to planning and execution.

In the case of your employees, planning takes on many angles and options. But, if you're listening to them with a shot and beer attitude you'll know what to do. Pay attention to what they say and treat them with respect and fairness and you'll find it all works out. Remember that all the decisions leading to a solid, stable company are also best for the employees. If the company grows and remains profitable the employees also benefit.

Managing Managers

Well, you made it. You worked hard and followed all the rules for planning and execution. Or perhaps you just got lucky. Many times, it's a combination of both if you're a successful manager. The guy who says luck had no part in his success is just plain wrong. If you're a passive manager it's almost a sure thing you are following the path of other passive managers who held this position before you. There are so many passive managers in business today that gaining a position is usually just one of them promoting someone with a style just like theirs. People like other people who are like themselves….and there you go.

But, nothing changes the fact that you're now a boss, a big boss. You have some number of managers or directors reporting to you. Each of those people have supervisors under them and they in turn have employees under them. With any luck you're not in a company with even more layers of management, but then again, passive managers like multiple layers of management. It suits their style of management being separated from the action. As I've mentioned several times, passive managers can think of ideas, they can create plans (although they may not be grounded in the reality of day to day work) and they can create a reporting structure which looks good on paper. But, they cannot execute! And by that, I mean they have a very difficult time monitoring the performance of any plan and making the changes that modify the "thinking Plan" into a "working plan".

First of all, you have to decide where you want the company to be in five years. This is a "rolling five years", so each year you have to still be looking out five more. Failure to do this step is a critical flaw and will bring down the company.

Second you have to decide what it's going to take to achieve your goal. Generally. this is a multi-point answer taking into consideration marketing, sales, production, delivery and above all quality and customer satisfaction. Failure to give any one of these functions the attention they require will also lead to a critical issue.

So, now you know these two answers and most importantly you know they will have to be revisited continuously to make them work as planned. It's time to meet your management team.

First let's talk about setting the tone. Have each department head, let's call them directors, explain what his department does, its size and make up, what its objectives are, where they stand on meeting those objectives and what they predict for the next 18 months. This presentation should be by each director, while standing up front with all the other directors present. On one hand you're looking for insight into how each department operates and what exactly the focus is now and should be going forward. But, much more importantly, you're looking at the directors' style. Does he really know his department or is he telling you the high-level babble he has gotten away with for years? Does he have a focus on what makes the company great or what makes their department look good? And what "needs" does he see for the future to grow or perhaps keep up?

The manager who plans and executes is going to come across to you as someone who has or is trying to get every efficiency out of the existing workforce and only asks for what it will take to grow based on those improvements. This manager talks about steps he takes based on "the company's" needs and not based on his own department. Odds are you'll find most directors, the passive ones, telling stories of how they plan to increase production and quality by growing the workforce and/or adding software assistance. They never see managing the processes with the existing workforce as an answer.

A great strategy is to grill the first director by asking questions about details. How do you know your group is efficient? When did you last take a look at your efficiency? How did you evaluate your efficiency? How can you reduce your budget and improve your productivity? With every answer it usually opens up other questions along the lines of these examples. You're just making the point, to all the directors at once, that this is your style and these are the important points they all should be able to speak about.

After the first director is finished, take a break. Go off by yourself and let them talk about what's happening. Most likely the rest of the director presentations will go the same way but you've set the tone. They now understand what you focus on. But, don't make the major mistake of dropping this after the meeting. Schedule one on one sessions to follow up on these presentations in quick fashion. Make certain everyone knows, crystal clearly, that your idea is to improve productivity, improve quality and lower cost. AND make sure they know you don't want one of those three, but that you want them ALL at the same time. Remember, you're a manager who gets things done, you don't put up with half-baked answers which produce a whole lot of what you always got. This is going to be a huge change, they're not going to like it and they're going to resist you. Be prepared to deal with that and if needed you'll have to rather quickly cut one loose to make the point.

    Let me say here that if your situation is one of being the existing manager this might be a major style change. It will represent a complete departure from what you've been doing up until now. But being a manager who gets things done means you change to meet the needs or conditions you see. There's nothing wrong with making a statement about "going in a new direction" or "changing the process of how we focus and report". Don't hesitate making changes, even core operational changes, because it will be so new and different from what was done in the past. A manager who gets things done views change and adjustment as necessary, reasonable management opportunities.

    This same strategy applies to your personal life. You may find that making major changes in the way you handle your personal life is a good thing. Maybe you come to realize spending more time with your spouse and/or family is a positive change. Maybe you'd like to spend weekends with your spouse and should make arrangements to be able to do that. Maybe those school functions you could have attended but didn't is something you feel you should change. Just because you haven't done things like this before doesn't mean it's not a good thing to try.

Budgets are a good thing. No person or business runs effectively without a budget. And, most of the time, every company spends a lot of time and energy creating their budget. Usually this is done department by department so that it can be rolled up into the company budget. I see this as the critical flaw in company design. The problem is that no overall performance objective is set. They just set a budget objective and each department has to submit a budget to ensure they'll be able to do their part to achieve that goal. What a crappy way to go about it and here's why.

Each department manager builds his projection of needs on a target of production he feels safe with. As he gathered data from the managers, if he bothered, each manager made sure he only submitted goals he could reach. This is done just in case the goals become actual objectives he has to meet. Then the director trims that goal a little to ensure he can't fail. What you end up with is a budget that's failproof from the director's point of view. The company wasn't part of the consideration from an efficiency standpoint. All the company provided was the budget target. Then each department came up with what it would take to get there from each department's viewpoint.

Now, reading this you surely might think it can't be like that. But consider this: How many times have you heard someone in management say "we have to spend this money by the end of the year or we won't get the same budget next year." The budgeting process is complete crap. No one ever looked at the overall process to see what's needed and what could be eliminated or improved. No one ever said "I'll do more in my group with fewer people and you'll have more money for your group to do what it needs." That's not the way company organizations are built today.

Nugget: Work groups have individual departmental goals which conflict with or even work directly against doing things better. I do what's good for my department even though it adversely impacts your department. Good for me and screw you. And even more ridiculous is upper management going along with this program, even establishing the objectives which are counterproductive. Sounds impossible………happens every year and every day in the business world.

Nugget: Department heads are often paid more, to some extent, on the number of employees in their group. The theory is it must be more difficult to manage more people so the larger the group the higher the salary or bonus should be. What bullshit! The unintended result of this thinking is to have department heads incentivized to add people. There isn't any incentive to be more efficient, eliminate duplication or redundant work steps. This is just one example of how logical reasoning produces the exact behavior you would hope to eliminate. It would be a much better approach to base a bonus or raise on a decrease in departmental budget while raising or maintaining productivity levels. That's an achievement worthy of a reward.

The company is the entity not the department. You can't have objectives for any of the pieces if they don't directly work to improve the company as a whole. And this is why it's so important to know how work flows overall. If you break down the process of workflow into what happens in each department it's bad. Why? Because each piece is then treated as the end result. You will create objectives for department A which hinder department B from doing a better job. It can't be avoided and will surely happen if you look at work processes in a compartmentalized way.

Now, let's not get too fidgety and think the big boss is a person who knows everything and only has directors in place for show. That's not true. He cannot and will not be able to know the process flow details. But anyone worth his pay will know what questions to ask to be comfortable that the right steps are being taken.

A good start is to request a budget proposal that meets your productivity increase goals and cuts 10 percent from this years' costs. A good start is to have directors submit joint budgets that cover the work performed in their departments as a whole.

If you ask a director why it takes this amount or this much time to produce a piece of stuff……..you want an answer. You don't want to hear "that's what it takes", or "you don't understand the process", or "it's always taken this long". You need to hear what's been done to figure out the steps, if all of them are even needed, what collaboration has been done between departments to streamline the process. And finally, what improvement has already been made. Don't allow yourself to be guided by smooth talking directors who think they've seen your kind before and just need to stall you long enough to meet your replacement.

Nugget: most mangers don't ask the hard questions. Maybe they don't want to embarrass anyone, maybe they don't want to be seen as not knowing the answer, maybe they feel they don't have time. Or, worst of all, maybe they like the person and don't want to make them look bad. COWCHIPS!!!

This isn't a fraternity. You're not their pal, their buddy or their friend. You're their boss. If you don't act like it because of some personal reason; you need to be replaced and have them bring in someone who can do the job.

The company is what you're supposed to be managing not a personal relationship. Grow a pair, pull up your big boy pants and do your job.

Now, it's the perfect time to say "hey, you don't mention how I'm supposed to manage our stock price, our global marketing image, our research and development effort and all the things any good management school will teach. You're right, this book will not lead you in any of those directions. And yes, you'll need talent and skill to manage those issues to be a completely successful manager at any company.

But, you can do all those things and fail. If you don't grasp how to manage your people, how to get things done, how to execute, then all of what you learned or thought about leading a successful company is Bull!! Again, what happened to the steel industry, the American Automobile industry and any number of large, can't fail, companies that built this country. They all failed or lost customer confidence, product quality, market share and importance.

You have to know your people. No, not every single person in the company but you have to know what they think as a group. Are they aware they have a voice? Are they aware their suggestions count? Do they know management values them and understands they know more about the day to day than any of the management team?

It's a culture. It's a feeling we're all in this together from the top manager to any employee you can think about. Certainly, you don't want employees walking into your office to chat every time they have an issue or suggestion.

But by the same token you want them to know, from examples, that anytime they have a reason to talk with management, they'll be heard. Culture is top down not bottom up. And the biggest mistake you can make is not setting the tone. Not making sure your managers follow this plan. Never lose sight of the fact that people lie, or at least color the story to reflect what you want to hear. It takes probing questions, follow-up and yes

ACTION. Action to unquestionably demonstrate you mean what you say and BACK IT UP. Don't get complacent with your management team. They will drift if you give them a chance.

Lets' talk about training for just a little. Obviously, there are two kinds of training, job specific training and company culture training. Almost everyone understands job specific training. But few realize how company culture training really occurs.

I've seen the same action take place so many times it's nauseating. A new person comes into a department. Usually it's a person new to the company but it also applies to a person who's been with the company and is being moved or promoted. They report that first day and get their assignment overview. "you'll be doing (whatever) and here's how you'll get trained to do that (some explanation that fits the job). Maybe the training is to observe someone doing the job for a few days or maybe the person is reading an outline of the processes and actions to be followed to do the job. It doesn't matter. What the person, who showed up bright eyed and bushy tailed, realizes is no one really cares if they work for eight hours or not. They've immediately, without anyone realizing it, been taught company culture or at least a version of it.

I've observed that most of the time when a new employee arrives the job has not been defined as an eight-hour job. Either no one spent the time to think the tasks through or they assumed "down time" is part of the normal day in that position. But, what does the new employee see. They are being taught that not working all the time is ok. They're being taught the boss is ok with you having periods of time where you can just sit. People are very creative and perceptive and once they realize the rules they immediately find options to fill gaps or take advantage of the rules. That's human nature.

I have observed companies whose employees work on computers all day. They perform tasks using programs to complete work. By the nature of the work there are down times or periods when the "job" is put on hold. But no one has looked at this issue and found alternative work to be performed during these periods. So, like any good, intelligent individual the employees begin personal emails, visiting web sites and in general spending their time on personal "work". And who suffers for this poor management, the business. It wouldn't be easy to create a productive alternative for this situation. And it would be even more complicated to monitor actions so that alternative company business was being performed instead of personal business. But, that's managements job! I agree, it's not easy. It takes thought and a monitoring strategy to ensure policy is being followed. But it's critical and has to be done.

What you end up with if you don't address these situations is an employee who doesn't even think they're doing something wrong. This is the way we work. I'm not goofing off; the boss knows what's going on and it's ok. This is passive management at its core. Not only does the company spend much more than is needed to get work completed, but it has to pass on this cost to its customers.

And, it's sad to say, but in every case where this situation exists you will find that quality is not where it needs to be. Any management structure that allows this situation to exist will also accept poor quality work. The act of overlooking the monitoring of process efficiency is almost always coupled with overlooking the monitoring of the quality of employee performance. So, what you get is not only poor performance but poor-quality work. And not because of the employees but because of management.

    I'm not saying you have to have every employee working constantly for eight hours or you're doomed. In fact, that can rarely happen. But you have to make sure jobs are thought through and planned. When someone needs more help, you should never make the assumption the additional person will be doing the same things the existing people in that job are doing. Three people being busy enough to require help doesn't mean four people will be busy all day. First, can we improve on the processes the existing people use? If help is needed is it for a full day, partial day, certain periods of the day or what? And, most importantly, how will this person spend his/her day to provide the best benefit for the company. If we move someone into this group and we need occasional help during the day, what do they do all day? Do not build an eight-hour position out of a job that takes fewer hours. It's easy, it's comfortable and it's very wrong.

    Any new person in almost any position in a company will see things with a different prospective. As a manager you should take advantage of this situation and get their viewpoint. While they're learning the job or while they have free time you want to get their input.

The Shot and Beer Manager

Assign them to outline how tasks flow, how work moves, where they see questions or problems. This task serves multiple purposes. It gives the employee time to organize and understand how they see the job. And it gives management a chance to see how the process is viewed, what appears as roadblocks or hinderances to something more efficient. New people aren't tainted by how things "should" go. They see things from a clean viewpoint and may just turn up a nugget of value which was previously overlooked. In any case, nothing was lost by having them tasked with this free time filler.

Example: A person started at a large company in the mail room. There was a hiring push going on and several people were being hired but couldn't be moved to their "real" position immediately so they were spread around entry level departments until decisions could be made to distribute them. In itself this wasn't a bad strategy because the hiring process took quite a bit of time. So, people were being added and temporarily held in entry level spots. While working in the mailroom there wasn't enough work to keep busy all day. The mail process of sorting and distributing might have taken ten people but there were eighteen people assigned to work there. The managers of the mailroom didn't make any adjustments to their processes. It was "ok" for several people to sit around doing nothing. It was ok for some people to skip a delivery route since more than the number needed were assigned to that route. Coming into the company this was the worst way to start employees. While being in the mailroom was not the position they were hired to do, they were being trained in company culture. Sure, it would be different once they were promoted out and got to a job more in line with their abilities. But, by then, the next manager had to deal with the impression already created. These new employees had been shown, by example, that the company wasn't always concerned with getting eight hours work for eight hours pay. Sure, most of these employees turned out to be just what the company wanted them to be. But, they never forgot their initial culture training. They always knew the bottom line, if you didn't work all day it's ok.

How to Approach Process Change

We've talked a lot about things to focus on and how to be careful to see the overall process picture. You definitely want to understand what each piece of the process does before you start changing the way different parts of the process are done. The biggest mistake you can make is two-fold: not understanding how your change will affect other parts of the process is usually the first mistake. The second is not recognizing your error and letting the change you made adversely affect other parts of the process for too long. Both of these errors happen often and not only don't correct a problem but because employees see the ineffectiveness of your changes their attitude deteriorates. Now you end up with no process improvement and employees who have less desire to do what it takes to work through or around the issues you've caused.

So, what are you looking for when you look at the processes involved in doing the job. It's actually quite simple. Start from the position that each employee, no matter what his job or set of tasks are, should be able to start work and end his day without the need to ask any other employee for help or information or be held up from his normal pace. In other words, he should be able to work at his own speed all day long completing his tasks exactly as expected without the need to interrupt his routine because he had to wait or ask for information from another employee. Anytime one employee has to wait and/or contact another employee to get some piece of information they need before they can complete or continue their part of the job it is a waste of time for both employees.

Well you say…..that can't be true. And you use two examples to point this out. First, field people have to contact the office people to give them updates about what's being done or has been done. And second, sales people have to contact the office to communicate specific details about a sale so the customer will be completely satisfied. Therefore, the premise about company people talking to each other as a waste of time is wrong. And to that I say: Nay, Nay. Is that really true or are you just stuck in the traditional way you've always thought of how things should go? For instance, couldn't the field person complete an electronic ticket of his status, automatically letting the office know what's going on without any personal contact? Couldn't sales fill out a contract, possibly electronic, that captures the details of each sale without a personal interaction to explain those details each time?

Example: there was a company where the field people had to find information from a group in "the office" and when that occurred, they made the call. They called so many times the office people couldn't get their normal work done on time. On top of that many times when they called there was no one available to answer the call and the field people had to wait and call back later, doing nothing in the meantime. To resolve this issue the office group manager decided to designate a person full time to answer phones and resolve questions and relieve all the others in the group from having to answer phones. This worked fairly well and most of the time the field person got an answer and moved on. There were still times when the phone was busy and people had to wait. But, overall, the process change was better and things ran smoother than before by just devoting a person, full time, to answer the questions.

The real problem here wasn't the field people needing answers or the fact that the "office" had the answers. The real problem was the field should have had access to the answers directly and eliminate the need for the call in the first place. But that was just too much of a step for anyone involved to see. It had always been the practice for the office to have access to the system where the answers were kept. No one ever considered giving access directly to the field people and let them do their job, on their own, all day without the call.

And this is why you have to look at the overall process. Do things really have to be done the way they've been done in the past?

Another issue is using temporary or occasional help to solve a spike in your workload. When you do this think the situation all the way through. Are you going to get everything you need or are you stopping short of your goal? Have you figured out how to get the most from the time and money it will take to use this option?

Example: A company uses a third-party company to complete some jobs during periods of heavy demand. It works well and allows the company to only have the number of permanent employees that are necessary most months of the year. The third-party company knows the routine and requirements of the jobs they're assigned and completes the work with good quality. However, when the work is completed it has been done in a system that's not used by the host company. When the completed work is passed back to the host company it must devote some period of time to recording the completed work in the operating system they use. It's always been done this way and even though the delay in making this information available in the company system causes problems, it's just the way it is.

The real problem here wasn't the use of the third-party company. That worked well and solved a problem. The actual problem was no one ever considered having the third-party company complete their work in the same system the host company used. Yes, it sounds simple but it was outside the thinking parameters of the host company managers. And for years they did each job twice when it came to recording the completion information. Even though the delay in converting this new information caused problems down the road no one ever looked at that issue to see how it could be corrected. No one took the time or thought the process through to see how they could avoid having this issue come up every time they used the third-party company.

It sounds ridiculous when you look back on some of these situations. It's the last thing you would expect to have happen or to be let go for so long. But this always happens and I'm sure situations like this exist in many, if not all, companies today.

    Example: A company who had service people in the field was having a problem. They found that when technicians arrived at a customer location they sometimes needed additional information. In many cases the additional information wasn't going to be ready for the better part of an hour so they dispatched the technician on another job in the meantime.

    The problem they wanted to correct was all the driving time and fuel used to do the extra driving. The solution they arrived at was to have the technician stay at the original location and wait for the information. That way the extra driving time and fuel would be eliminated. However, the original customer was billed for the time the technician was waiting for information and each invoice went up by the cost of the extra time. While driving time and fuel went down, customer bills went up and customer satisfaction went down. Here the thought process was faulty. While the solution solved one company departments problem it made the customer satisfaction results much worse. It's not that the problem didn't need to be solved. It's that the solution didn't accomplish the goal which always includes creating a better experience for the customer. The option of having the technician look up their own information or having the information on the original dispatch ticket didn't come up during the resolution phase of the problem. The first option considered was to eliminate the extra driving and that change was not in the best interest of the customer.

This is the classic case of not thinking the impact of a change all the way through. What's good for one department isn't always the best solution for the company.

Duplication……aahhh there couldn't be duplication done in any company. That would be completely wasted time and surely cause some confusion by having more than one set of records for the same information.

Sorry, this happens all the time. Each work group believes they have some significant information that's needed for their part of the job and they have to track that information in their own way. So, they create a set of records separate from the "master" file. They have much the same information but with a few details that apply just for their groups purposes. Whenever a new account or a change to an existing account happens these auxiliary records are updated…..most of the time. And the net result is you have information about an account which is different depending on where you look. This situation is irresponsible for any management team to allow. Whatever the reason for the interest in "special or specific" information might be it has to be addressed in the master account and not in any separate or duplicate record. In todays' electronic world correcting this situation is easy and has multiple answers. But continuing to have the problem should not be a choice.

Another problem is different departments doing the same work over that another department already did.

The Shot and Beer Manager

The information gathered by one department should never have to be gathered or recorded again by any other department. But, more often than not it happens and sometimes more than once in the same company.

Many of these situations could be eliminated if only one electronic database was used in the company and each department had its own direct access to it. Anytime an employee mentions a file, database or set of records they keep in their department it's an opportunity to eliminate the need for that extra set of records.

Another situation that requires a serious look is quality. Quality is your driving force behind efficiency and time savings. If anything is going to adversely affect quality it's not a good idea. And many times, the impact of a change on quality is unknown and used as the reason to avoid changing how things are done. As you investigate options for changing the way you're doing things it's often brought up that any change will be bad for the quality of the product or service. In fact, that's usually because change itself is always viewed as bad and should be avoided. It's why passive managers survive without doing anything that makes significant improvement. It's the fear of making things worse instead of better.

Quality is your main objective. But that doesn't mean you can't change the way things are done. It means you have to think about the end to end process making certain the impact of the change works all the way through the process. Change gets a bad reputation because it's not done correctly. It's either not given enough thought to understand the entire impact of the change. Or, it's that change isn't modified as it's implemented to adjust for real world intricacies as it's installed. No matter how well you plan for the change, it's often necessary to modify it during implementation. If you don't recognize this and look for those necessary changes you will make the situation worse instead of better.

Looking for Process Change Opportunities

How are you going to find out if a process can be or needs to be changed? Here are the steps which work.
1. You're going to interview workers from each work group involved in what you see as "the process" to accomplish the production of some product or service. These interviews will be only with workers from each individual group without workers from other groups involved. Mixing work groups will stifle their replies and make them color their responses to cover for what they perceive as getting others in trouble. Many times, you'll hear something that adds a work group to the mix that you didn't think was involved in the process flow. In these cases, add an interview with that new group to your investigation. You want to fully understand just how the work, and therefore the issues, are involved with each work groups actions.
2. Decide who will do the interviewing of workers from the groups involved in your review. In some companies this may be done by you. But in many situations that would be impractical and another

manager will be doing the interviews. Make sure they understand how to do the interview, what questions to ask and how to make the people comfortable. Do not have the manager or supervisor from the group conduct the interview. They will be intimidating and protective which leads to no constructive information and no progress. Select someone not involved with that work group. The best choice is someone not involved with any of the work groups in the process you're investigating. That way the same person can conduct all the interviews and put together a comprehensive view of the overall workflow.

3. What questions should you ask. First explain the point of the meeting. It's not to find fault or look for a "culprit". This is a meeting to find out the details of how things work, what the people like and think works well, what they don't like or believe is time consuming, cumbersome or counter-productive to quality and/or customer satisfaction. It's their chance to provide input into how to make their job and the product better. Once they're comfortable with this premise, move on to asking process questions. What starts your job process? What information or material do you get, how do you know what to do, what does it take to do that and how do you move your part of the work along to the next group. This is the core of what you want to know. And I'm sure you can see why a neutral party is needed for the interview. Each answer generally generates its own follow-up

questions. All you want to know is "how do things go". There are no wrong answers and no feedback will get anyone into a problem or situation where you will condemn any of their actions. Don't be stupid. You want to know what's going on and that can't happen if you comment on or ridicule how the process is being done today.

4. Many times, one group will provide insight to problems in another group which you may not hear when you talk to that group. You have to probe and make sure you know which group has an issue and why that issue exists. If you've created the sense of comfort level required, this probing will be non-threatening and lead to the core of the problem or issue. Sometimes you'll have to go back to a group and ask a few more questions after you see the overall flow and need more detail to fully understand why things are the way they are.

5. You are NOT there to fix things during these interviews. Don't fall into the trap of hearing something you don't like and start making changes or getting irritated because the flow isn't what it should be. You're hearing the truth….document it and keep going.

6. Once you've completed your interviews with all the groups take the time to detail the flow and UNDERSTAND what happens and why. Only then can you start to think about process changes.

7. With the whole flow in mind (I like to see it on a white board with the end to end steps) make changes you think are needed and rework the flow

to ensure a good change here doesn't cause a bad effect there. Think this through several times and get input to ensure you are satisfied it will work as intended.
8. Get the entire group together who participated in the interviews. Explain what changes are about to happen and why. You may not address all the issues that were talked about, in fact the implementation plan will almost always be less than what at least one person in the group would like to see. But make sure everyone understands this is what's going to happen and their best position is to get behind the change.
9. Appoint a person to be in charge of the change and meet with him/her and their team regularly to determine the progress. Above all make whatever changes are needed to adjust the implementation to reality as necessary. Regardless of how carefully you thought the change through it will need to be modified to some extent as it's implemented. Do not shy away from making these changes. No plan will be perfect coming out of the design stage.

There are some cautions you need to be aware of. During the interviews you'll hear valuable, accurate issues to be addressed. You will also hear personal grievances or points of personal irritation. Know enough to see the difference. You'll also hear about issues which are very valid and should be corrected. But, they occur too seldom to justify a fix. Either the cost or the process disruption of the fix will be greater than you determine is reasonable.

If that happens, explain your position during the meeting where you outline the pending changes and move on. This is not a democracy where majority rules but employees need to know each idea was considered and why a decision was made. But, you're not looking for their consent.

Once implementation starts you'll need your backbone. Many employees and managers will resist change, that's natural. They'll do it passively and actively. Be aware of what might happen and be prepared to take it on. Don't work around anyone who doesn't want to change, address the issue as soon as it's identified. You have to make everyone who might be involved realize this change is going to happen. It might be adjusted, it might be modified and this might happen several times. But the change is going to happen and if you resist it for too long you may not be a fit at this company. This attitude about the change is a top down issue. You have to set the tone and enforce the change regardless of who is the obstacle. There will be bumps in the road which can be used as proof the changes can't work. Don't allow this. Investigate each obstacle, make the necessary adjustments and move forward.

One last caution, don't be so proud of wanting to make changes you refuse to admit it's not going to work and abandon the change effort. That would not be management with a plan and execution. If you've done your process change preparation correctly this shouldn't happen. But, if or when it does happen, that in spite of all your preparation this change isn't going to work out, admit it. Take the blame standing up. Get in front of your group and announce your decision. Point out some employees said it wouldn't work and they have proven to be right. Explain the company has learned from this effort and won't make the same mistake again. Don't be shy. Everyone knows it didn't work, stand up in front of your employees and admit it. Every employee needs to see that mistakes, while not what anyone wants, are openly admitted and not punished. When you do your best and things don't turn out it's still ok. You've learned a lesson and the company is better off for it.

    Now, many of you are going to read this section and think it applies only to large companies and not you or your situation. NOT TRUE. The outline works for anyone in any size company. If you are the owner and direct boss of your employees (remember size doesn't matter) this still applies. Of course, you have to adjust for the number of work groups and number of employees but it still works.

    Why not ask your people during a lunch break or down time "hey, does anyone have any ideas of how to make what we do better?" And, make sure they know you mean better for the customer and/or them as the workers. Sure, you've cut out some steps in the process I outlined but getting feedback is never bad. The old adage "two heads are better than one" was created for a reason. Everyone has a viewpoint and every viewpoint can either be a great idea or lead to a great idea. Often, you'll hear something that in itself isn't what you think needs to be changed but it will make you think of something that does. Use the employee resource and take advantage of their input. Different viewpoints are a good thing and managers who want to improve how things are done never pass them up.

    This highlights a major separation between passive managers and ones who get things done. The passive manager fears these direct employee interactions. They fear hearing ideas from their employees because they never want to make changes to a process or routine. While the idea may sound good and even appear to be something that would work, they avoid it. Remember, passive managers never take risks.

Examples and Nuggets

So now it's time to wrap up what I've been describing. At this point you might be thinking it's all been common knowledge or basic logic. Well, you could look at it that way. But, every day in businesses all across the United States every misstep and wrong move described in these pages is made over and over again. But why? It's not that these nuggets and examples are only known by the few who are more learned and wise than anyone else. No, no, it's the process of executing, being pro-active, having a plan and doing what moves you to that point on the horizon. These are easy to say actions but that's the problem, they're ACTIONS. I've pointed out several times most of the management people today are not only reluctant to take action……they fear it. It's exactly what separates managers who get things done from passive managers.

And now, if you've been paying attention, lets add a few more examples and nuggets to the list. These are all actions to consider and use whenever the situation presents itself; or, they're actions you should take to avoid some situations ever occurring.

A manager was well known among his management team for having meaningless meetings. It was an inside joke which employees never shared with the boss. He would schedule a meeting, usually have an agenda, and invite anyone who might be able to offer insight to the issue of the day. The problem was, and actually still is, the meeting would last for what would seem like forever. At the end, which was often only ending because everyone was burned out, there would be no conclusion, no decision. The result of the time spent huddled up in a room for an hour or more would be a second meeting was scheduled to discuss the same topic again. DO NOT BE THIS GUY. If you schedule a meeting have a plan. What input do you want, what do you need, what problem or issue are we resolving and above all: reach a conclusion……make a decision……….take ACTION. Remember you might be wrong but take the best shot. Don't keep walking up to the edge of the cliff……jump.

A guy starts a lawn care business and is successful. He's very personable, his work is good and always on time. He never does anything but the best-looking job. He felt he could cut 20 lawns a day but only three days a week. This is just a "part time" effort for him and he's a one man show.

So, he's making good money and grows to 75 customers meaning he's at 25 lawns to cut each of the three days he likes to work. But, it's too much. He can't cut 25 lawns each of the three days. And, there are rain outs or his personal schedule changes and he can't afford the extra time 5 extra lawns take each of his three work days. He could ride this out and change his goal but that would not get him where he wanted to be.

He made the only decision that made sense...he told 15 customers he couldn't handle them and had to quit cutting their lawns. Yes, he lost money. But it only meant he was where he saw himself from the beginning. And, it put him in a position to do a good job, every time for every customer. Making any other decision would have been wrong for his situation. It's perfect goal-oriented management.

A small deli owner hires a worker who can also bake pies. After a little while the worker suggests they start offering homemade pies and see how it goes. The owner looks into the cost of supplies and the time it would take to offer this additional option, and they begin. After just a few weeks the pies become a big hit and turn into a nice addition that draws more customers into the store. After some time goes by the pie baker abruptly leaves the store. The owner is high and dry when it comes to offering fresh baked pies. Many people ask for pies but while it's certainly profitable and a big customer draw, there seems no answer to how to replace the baker. A couple people come forward but they either can't create the quality or they just cost too much and don't like the working hours. So, after some soul searching the owner becomes the baker. There's much practice but after a couple weeks he's even better than the original baker and sales are better than before.

Will this kind of decision always work……..NO. But, it is an example of management executing a plan. The owner had the time and inclination to do the baking. And, while he never intended to do the job himself as a permanent solution, it worked out very well. Eventually he had every detail of the routine down perfectly and was able to train his own replacement baker, a person who met every qualification for being the baker but who had no baking skills. An example of management executing a plan. If you have the "point on the horizon" there are many ways to achieve it. Some will be better than others but not doing anything is always the poorest choice. Know your plan, remove roadblocks and achieve the objective.

All employees are human. They all do the same things and have the same hopes and dreams. You have to understand this logic: The employee will always color the explanation of a situation to put themselves in the best light. They're not being devious, they just see the explanation as a slight bending or small omission of what actually happened so they're not directly responsible for the outcome. And, so they tell their story to their boss. And the boss modifies this story, just a little, as they retell the explanation to their boss. And, so it goes. The farther from the actual event the more the explanation will be modified, sometimes ever so slightly and sometimes modified quite a bit. The manager has to understand this layer to layer deviation. Depending on the importance of the event, the follow up or inquiry into what happened has to be detailed. No reaction can be made and be truly effective and justified unless you know what the problem is that you're solving. At every level, ask questions in enough detail to be confident you understand the event. Now, you may understand it and it's still not the story you're hearing; that's ok. Sometimes your reaction doesn't have to depend on the story you heard as long as you know you're really correcting the "actual" problem. But ACT!

A company has a compensation plan which includes a bonus that's paid in February once the figures for the past year's performance are complete. The boss has a policy where only he signs checks and authorizes bonus payments. It's a fine plan so that he always knows the who and why for every employee. He's able to follow the logic of each manager/supervisor in deciding the level of bonus each employee will receive. But, the boss is busy and puts off the bonus check signing until he's able to review each case and approve the checks. Sometimes they get signed, according to the company plan, in February. But sometimes it might be March and once it wasn't until the first of April. This is the worst action a manager can deliver. Employees see the bonus payment as a guaranteed extra income source. They make plans and arrangements based on getting that bonus even though they're never certain of the amount, they know the schedule. From the employees' point of view the value the owner is putting on them is nothing. They feel he does not care about them and has no consideration for their feelings. This bonus should be a solid, positive demonstration of the company's value for each employees' contribution. Instead it becomes just another way to prove the company couldn't care less about employees. It becomes a gigantic negative and would be far better forgotten than paid the way it is. Employees are the life-blood of every company. Treat them and value them as equals in the business with each one contributing his/her share to the success of the company. You can SAY the right words as many times as you want but your ACTION is what creates the perception of your true feelings. Don't forget that.

There are many companies where the reporting structure is fake. While each employee may have a known or probable reporting structure, the actual fact, or perceived fact, is that the "big boss" is the only one they have to please. If you have or create a situation like this….get rid of it!! When you're a small enough business that you can walk around and directly have contact with employees, don't make decisions or changes without their direct manager. You have a reporting structure for a reason. If you belittle that structure you destroy not only the value of the manager but you destroy reaction to his instructions. Any direction he gives to his team will be put aside until the "big boss" validates the instruction. In effect you have a person in charge of the group who is only a clerk, not a manager. And, even though he gives direction…no real movement will occur until the group believes it's what is really wanted/needed by "the big guy".

Employee evaluations. We could probably write a book just about this issue. Not one person in any company would say this isn't a very important task.

They'd say it's critical for employees and managers alike. The problem is I cannot think of one company that does it correctly. Most fake it. Most fill the evaluation with feelings, impressions and estimates of effort and ability. In most if not all cases the evaluation is done halfheartedly, in a hurry without the thought and backup data it deserves. And this starts at the top and works its way down the management chain. DO NOT PERMIT THIS. Put measurable goals in place that actually mean something. Keep personal feelings and impressions OUT. Require that each employee has his evaluation according to the schedule you've all agreed to. Don't permit variations.

You will always hear there's no time. Don't put up with it. If it's important enough to have the process, then you must do the process. The lack of a valid, honest, timely evaluation process leads to a workforce perceiving the treatment of every employee as arbitrary and full of favoritism. It's the single most destructive policy in any company if it's not done the way it's supposed to be done. Admittedly it's not fun or easy. No one wants to deliver the bad news to an employee that he isn't working up to par. It's confrontational and can certainly feel bad. But, be proactive, set realistic, measurable, meaningful goals. And the key is to pick measurable goals.

If it doesn't matter, don't use it. One company had a section who's work assignments were based on completing tasks by an end date. So, if I had an assignment it needed to be complete and accurate by a date. I wasn't required to turn in time sheets every day and account for every hour. My performance as an employee was based on getting that work completed accurately by the date. And yet, my performance review always measured if I came in on time and left on time. Why? Be certain the measured tasks or categories actually mean something. What do we really pay this person to do? What do we expect from his performance routine? Why measure, and even care, about a category of performance that makes no difference to why we have the employee.

And, there is no reason to surprise an employee at the time of the performance review. If an employee is hearing about his poor or sub-par performance for the first time at the review, then you haven't done your job. Employees have to be kept aware of just how they stand. Do not permit or become part of a plan to "take action" about employee performance unless that employee has been kept up to date on how they're doing. That means no matter whether they're doing really well or not performing up to par, they must know during the performance period. You don't surprise them at a performance review. This is managements job to provide feedback that's informative and constructive. Your job is to take action that brings the employee up to the performance standard. You do not wait until a performance review to talk about any deficiencies.

Objectives. We could talk forever about the importance of setting objectives and just how basic they are to the well-run business. But the flaw almost always created is setting objectives that conflict with the intended outcome.

The rule here has to be that creating an objective is hard work and must be thought completely through. People are very creative and will find ways to meet the objective in some extraordinary ways.

Example: a company wanted to lower their inventory. They made that a key objective for the warehouse who is charged with maintaining an inventory of parts and material. Their objective was specifically to get the inventory lower and reduce company costs. So, the warehouse lowered their stock levels across the board.

At the same time the marketing and sales departments were tasked with increasing sales on optional items sold in conjunction with the main sale. It didn't take long at all before the installation department could not schedule and complete appointments without the necessary parts available in the warehouse each morning. Marketing & Sales were meeting their objective of increased orders and the warehouse was meeting its objective of lowering the inventory. But, the installation department was not even close to meeting their objective of installing orders within the objective window. As a defense the installation group began ordering "replacement" material, which appeared in a different category than "new" material. They kept track of this themselves, dispatched it each day to the installers who needed it and basically kept it off the radar of "new" material in inventory. A completely unsatisfactory resolution of their problem but the only choice they had to protect their department.

Was this a good arrangement for the company….NO. But once objectives are set the other departments objectives were not compatible with installation leaving them no choice.

So just like in the case of knowing the flow of work from beginning to end, you have to think objectives through. How does something that appears to be a straight forward objective actually impact the business as a whole? What will the impact of this objective be in all the other departments of the company? A positive result in one department does not mean it's a positive result for the business as a whole. You must think it through and at the minimum discuss the objectives with all the departments in a room at the same time. This is best done after forwarding them the proposed individual department objectives so they have time to think them through.

Every person God makes gets angry. Just because you're a boss does not mean you can say or do whatever you want any time you want to. Sometimes someone, anyone, will commit an act you deplore. Even if the employee has committed a grievous error, you can't take him to task in front of a group. I've worked for bosses who would find out something they didn't like during a conversation with an employee. It didn't matter who the employee was or where the conversation was taking place. It could be a manager or an employee. The boss would raise his voice and in no uncertain terms chew out the employee. He did not care who was around. This is wrong!! While the conversation is not only deserved but necessary you have to have it in private. You might have the person's manager there, you might have a Human Resources person there. But you do not have that conversation in public, never, at no time.

Employees are very important to each business. Show them their value. You most likely will not like each employee. You very likely will not want to be around some employees because their personality doesn't make you comfortable. But, that doesn't mean they don't have valuable comments to make and important information to provide. Put aside your feelings and listen. It might be painful but you have to do it, at least some of the time. No one understands the day to day processes of getting the work done more than the workers. If any manager tells you differently they are wrong and you might want to watch the manager more closely for a while. Evaluate every suggestion and understand it's value and possible impact. If you can't, then have someone investigate it and provide his review. And it's critical, as mentioned before, to always get back to the person with your answer or feedback.

Delegate. It's very easy to see the value in delegating tasks to others. The explanation for doing this is easy to follow and logically sound. But, few can actually execute delegating. Why you ask. It's easy to get a lot of things done by having some of the tasks done by others. True grasshopper. But now you're talking about trust. Yes, the delegator has to trust that others can and/or will do the task satisfactorily. And that is the problem. It's not the person who the task would be delegated to...the fault lies with the delegator. That person never took the time to develop his subordinates into a group he could trust. And unless he gives them a chance to learn, nothing will change and what can be done will be limited to what the boss can do himself. People have to learn and the only way they'll learn is by having a chance and doing. Each time someone reports on a task he has done it's another opportunity to bring them up to your standard. Let them fail. Let them return a task not completed as you intended. Point out the shortcomings, send them back to do it again, give them the chance to get better.

Project Evaluation. Regardless of whether a project has gone well or poorly you have to have a discussion about how that happened. What worked, what didn't work. What happened by plan and what was just an accident. In almost all cases this is not done when a project goes well. There's just as much opportunity to learn from a good job as one that's gone poorly. Don't pass up the opportunity to learn. Get the key players together and discuss the "why" of the project outcome. Good or bad you want to understand exactly why the outcome was the way it was. This is overlooked in too many cases. When the project worked out well everyone just walks around smiling and congratulating each other. But there are always lessons to be learned, things to be aware of, and pitfalls to be avoided. Make it a plan, don't let it be an accident that projects end just as you'd want. Yes, analyze every project that ends poorly. But don't fail to learn from the ones that go smoothly.

Time for a Shot and Beer?

By now you must realize the title of The Shot and Beer Manager does not refer to a drinking habit. It's all about your attitude towards managing your life and the people around you or working for you. You will find taking a straight-forward, no-nonsense approach to managing is a path to success. If you have a degree in business or just find yourself in a management position (actually everyone is managing at least their own life) you want to use your business knowledge and/or common sense in the best possible way. You want to be able to execute a plan and execute changes to a plan. In short, your success will be entirely based on your ability to take what you want to do and make it happen.

You will find most managers are threatened by this style. They may have good ideas but have limited or even no skill at turning those ideas into functioning processes. They can't execute and therefore the idea of "change" or initial implementations scare them. Do not be this kind of manager.

The Shot and Beer Manager relies on the ability to implement ideas. He can identify the passive managers and use them to his advantage. This is done by weighing every idea or comment they put forth against the fact that they dislike change, the unknown and confrontation. And, if you keep that in mind you can logically place a value on their contribution in every discussion.

The Shot and Beer Manager doesn't just ask questions. He asks questions until he's satisfied he knows what is going on. He asks questions until anyone trying to mask the truth has been exposed. He asks questions to ensure no one is saying or doing things that hinder the operation. He is not looking for friends. He is looking for success in whatever he's trying to accomplish.

Managing is hard. If you think you can ever get to a point in managing people where they'll know exactly what to do in every case….you're wrong. You'll change and so will they. You'll want more, you'll want deeper details, they'll forget how they did things the last time. Managing is a never ending, continuously evolving process. Mix into it the complexity of each individual's personality and it will sometimes feel like you will never get where you want to be. But, never forget…have a plan, execute, revise, execute…….repeat.

About the Author

Al joined the United States Naval Reserves at the beginning of his senior year in high school. After graduation he went on active duty and spent almost three years aboard the USS Vigor. After being honorably discharged he began a career working in the telecommunications industry for 38 years. Al started working as a coin collector for Bell of Pennsylvania, held several positions and was promoted to supervisor four years later. While working at Bell, Al attended the University of Pittsburgh School of General Studies (night school) and received a Bachelor degree in Psychology. During his working career he held multiple supervisory and staff positions and retired as a Process Re-engineering Manager with Bell Atlantic. He then spent 6 years as the General Manager of an Independent Telephone Company in Pennsylvania and subsequently worked as a Quality Manager and Process Engineer for Mapcom Systems. In addition, he and his wife spent 6 years as the owner/operators of an independent convenience store.

All of this experience along with multiple tales and adventures related to him by fellow managers and acquaintances have evolved into the examples, nuggets and recommendations contained in this book.

www.ingramcontent.com/pod-product-compliance
Lightning Source LLC
Chambersburg PA
CBHW052329220526
45472CB00001B/339